Black Europe

Arya Bàhram

Black Europe

Arya Bàhram

Black Europe

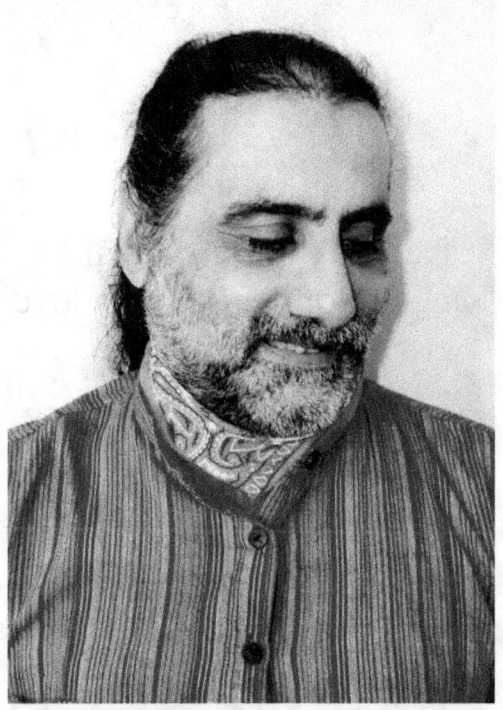

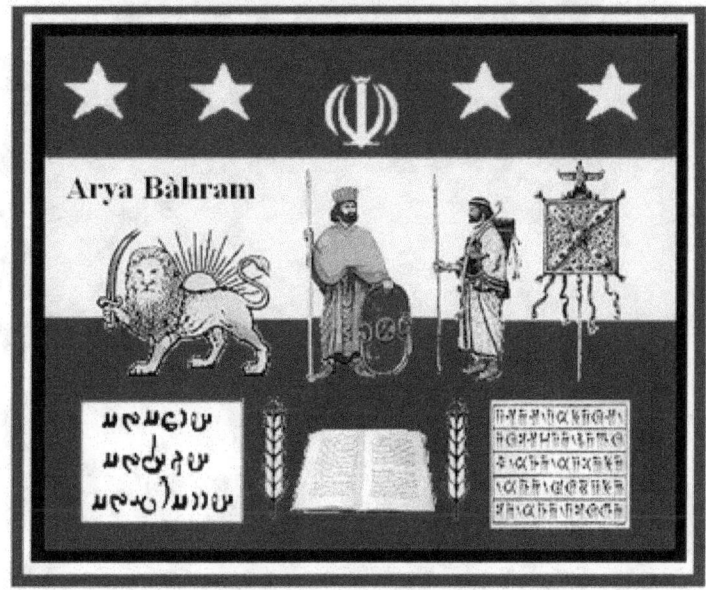

Musics for book - musiques pour livre - Musiken für Buch – آهنگها برای کتاب - Ahàng ha bàraye nibig ha

http://www.majidbahrambeiguy.at/my-foto-books---mes-livres-des-photos-.html

© Copyright 2016

Arya Bàhram (Majid Bàhram beiguy) , Österreich

Arya Bàhram

Black Europe

Dedicate to Barry White
King of Soul music with love

Arya Bàhram

Black Europe

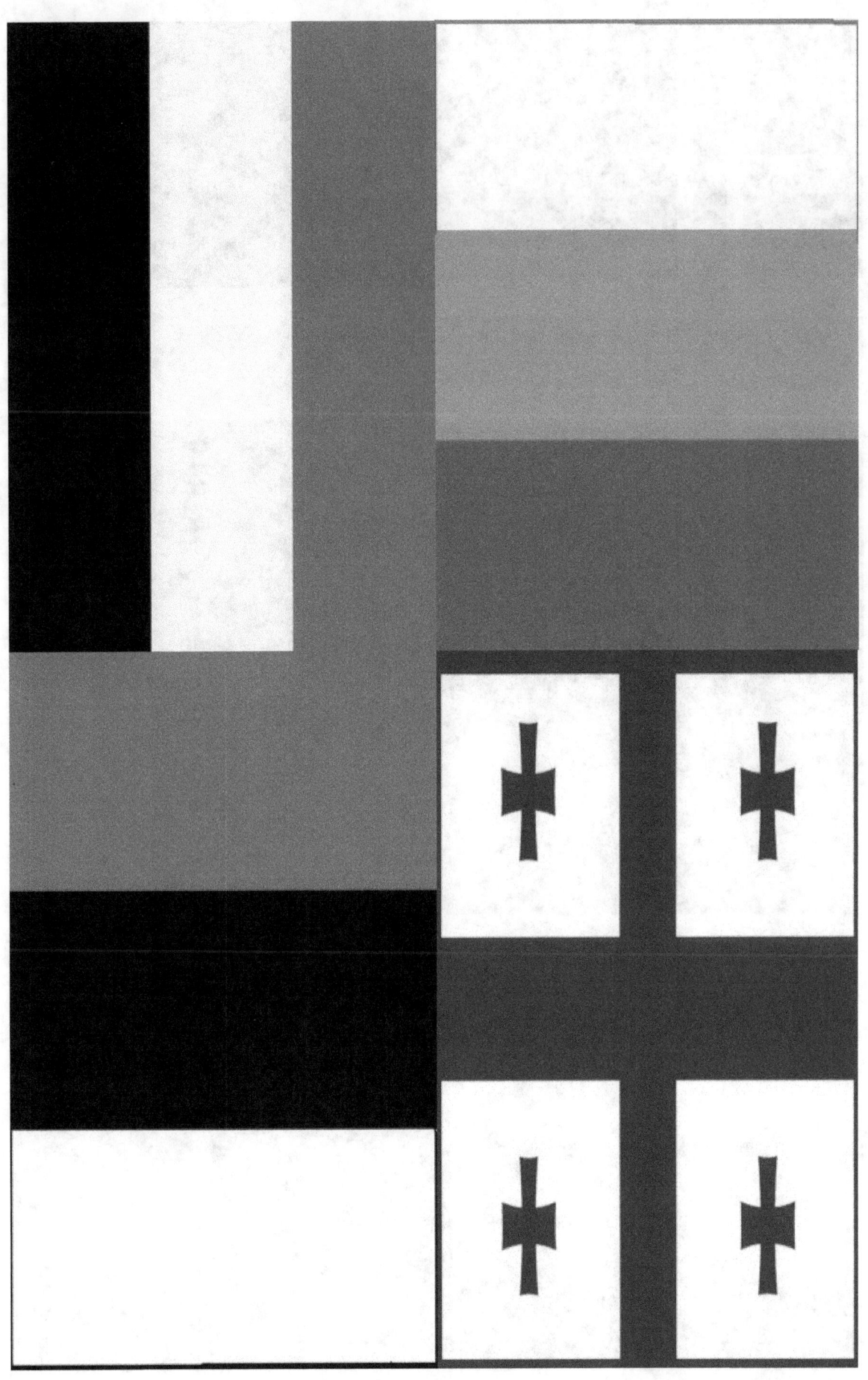

Arya Bàhram

Black Europe

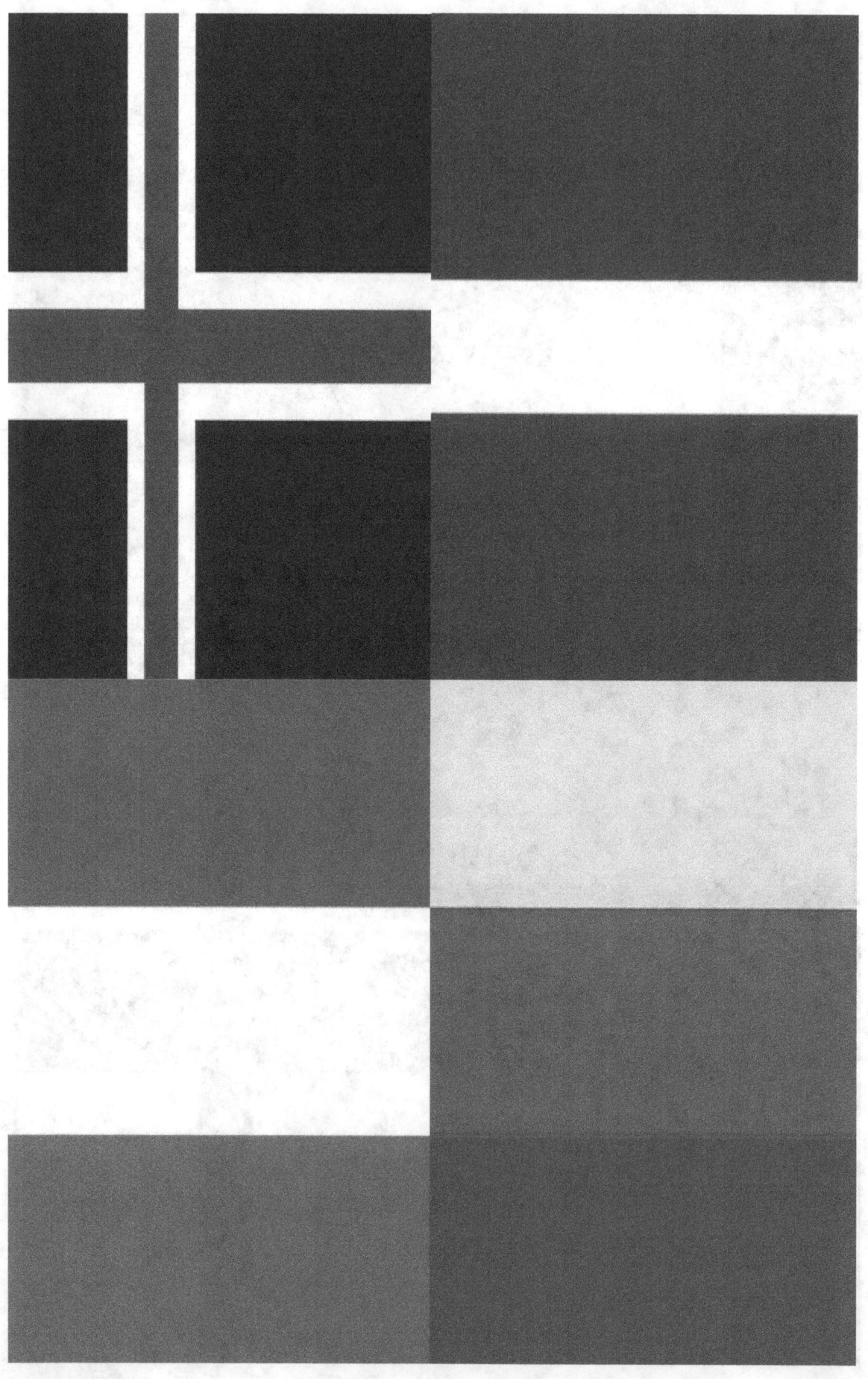

Arya Bàhram

Black Europe

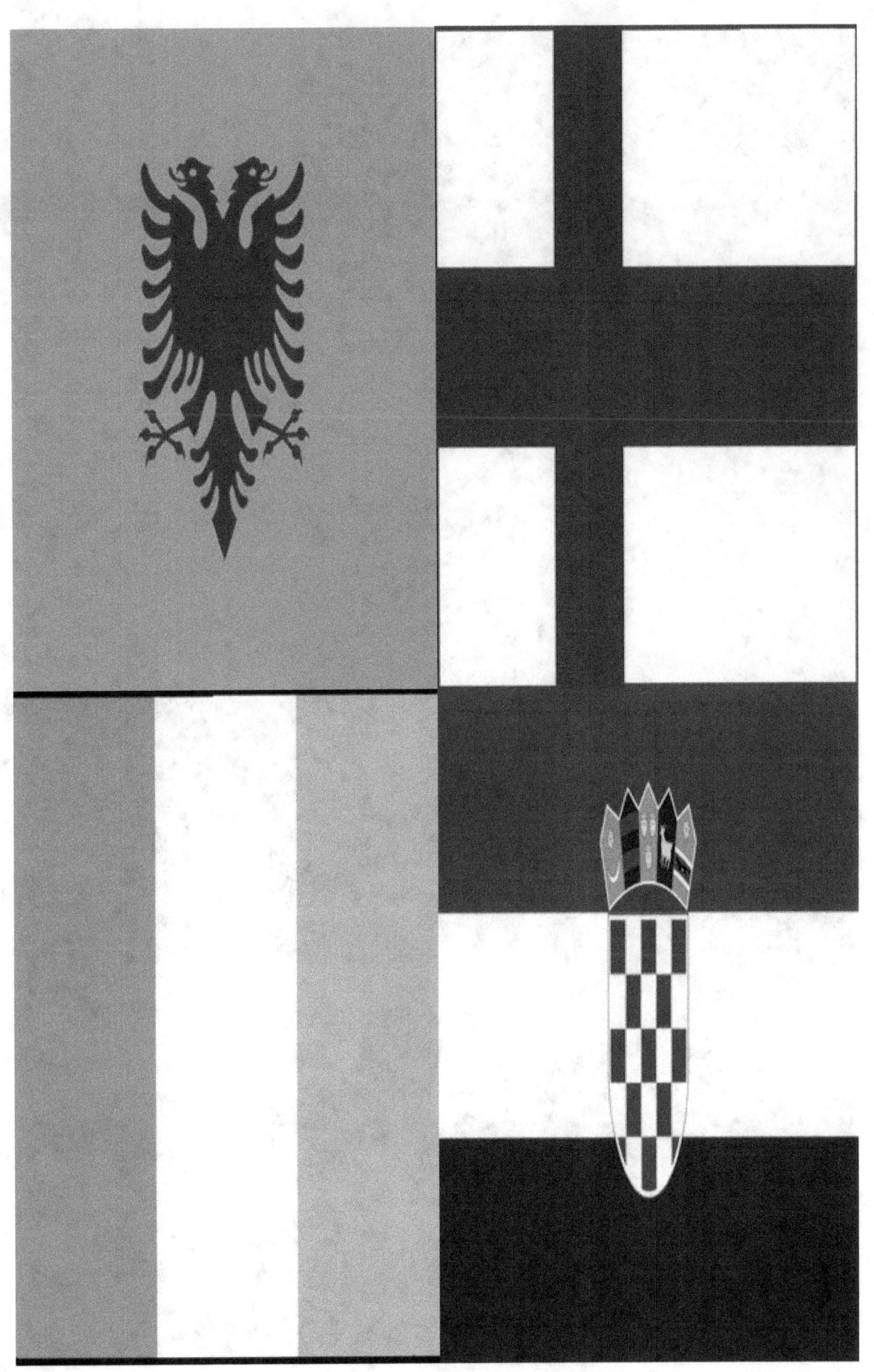

Arya Bàhram

Black Europe

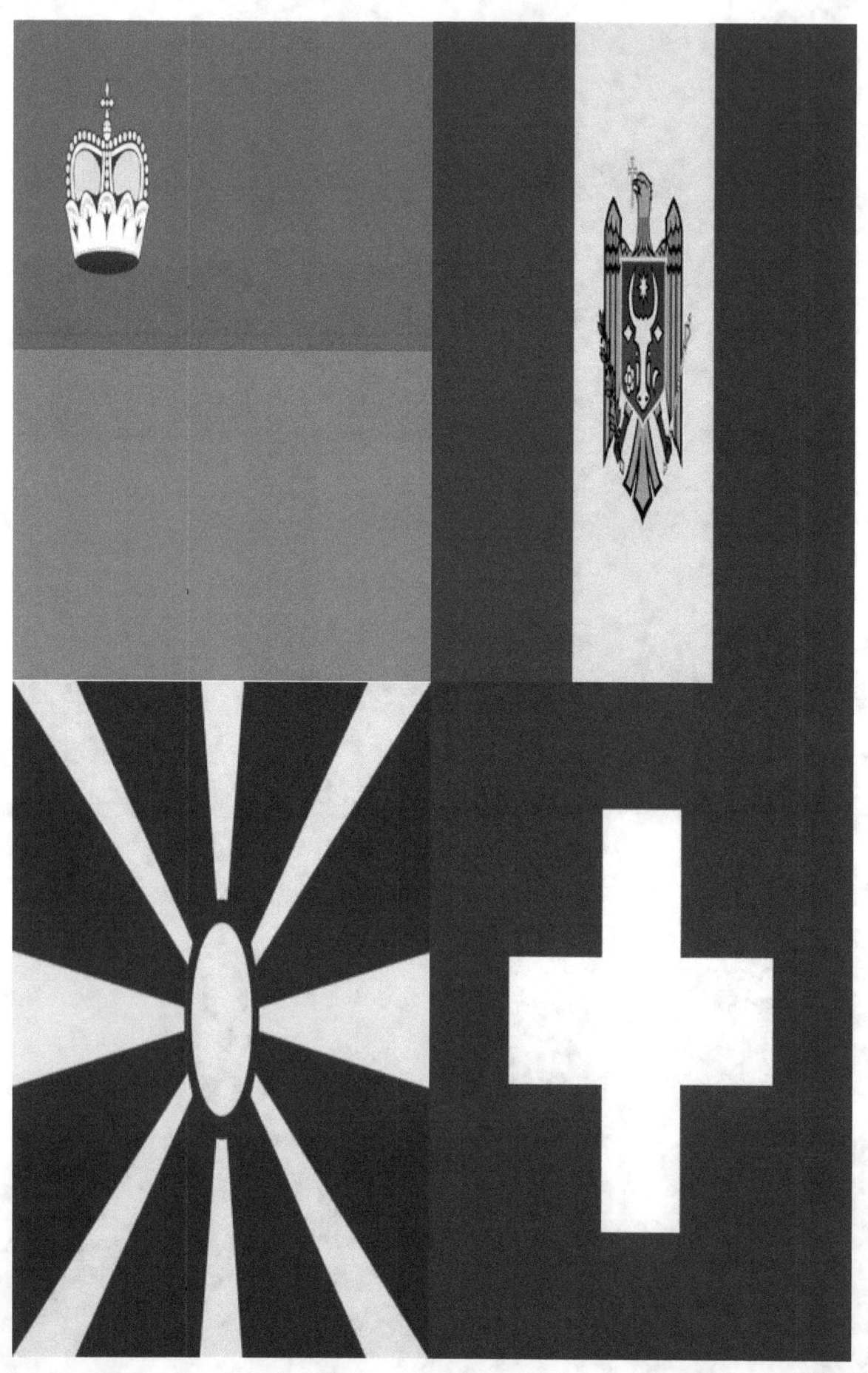

Arya Bàhram

Black Europe

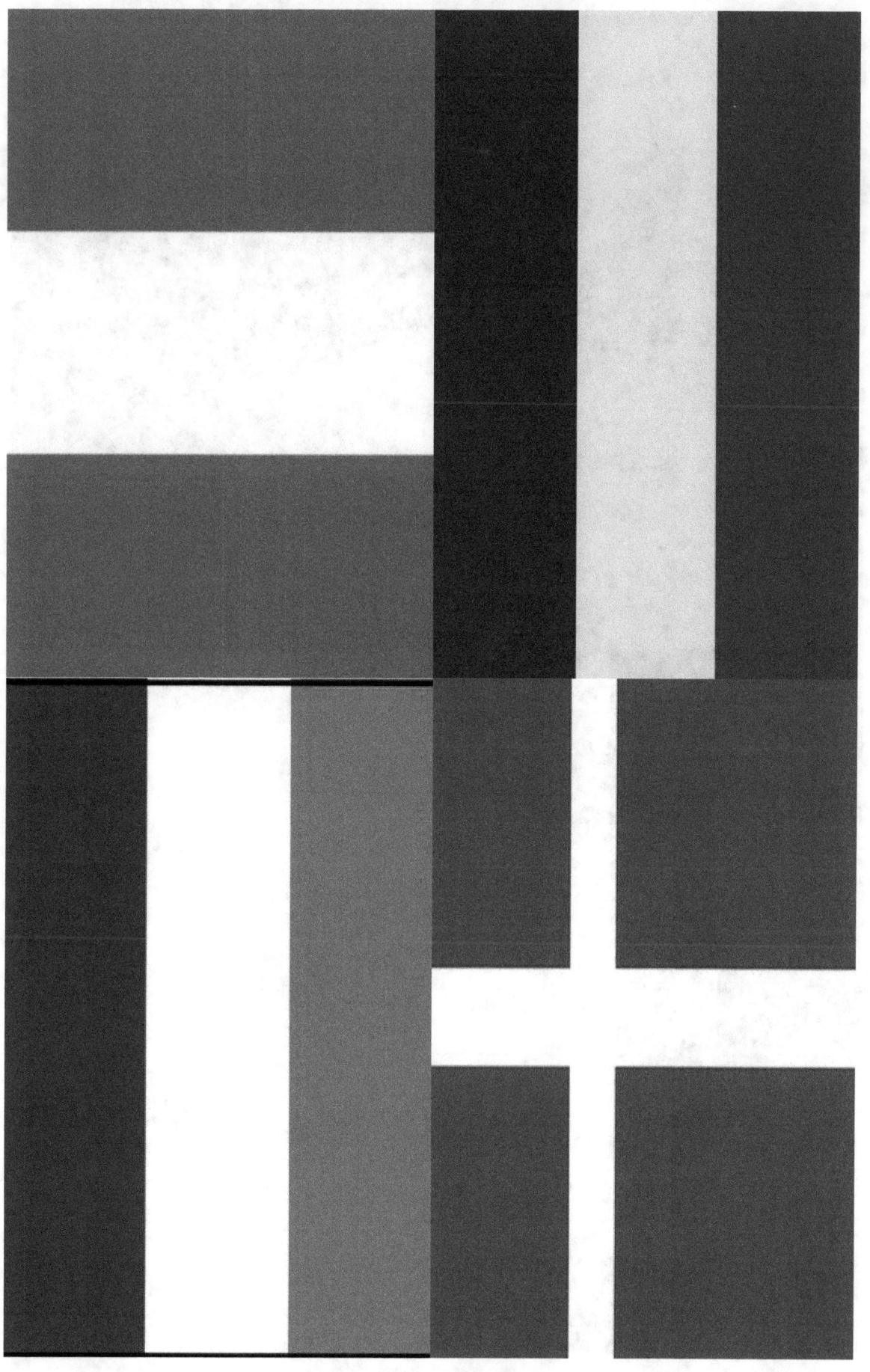

Arya Bàhram

Black Europe

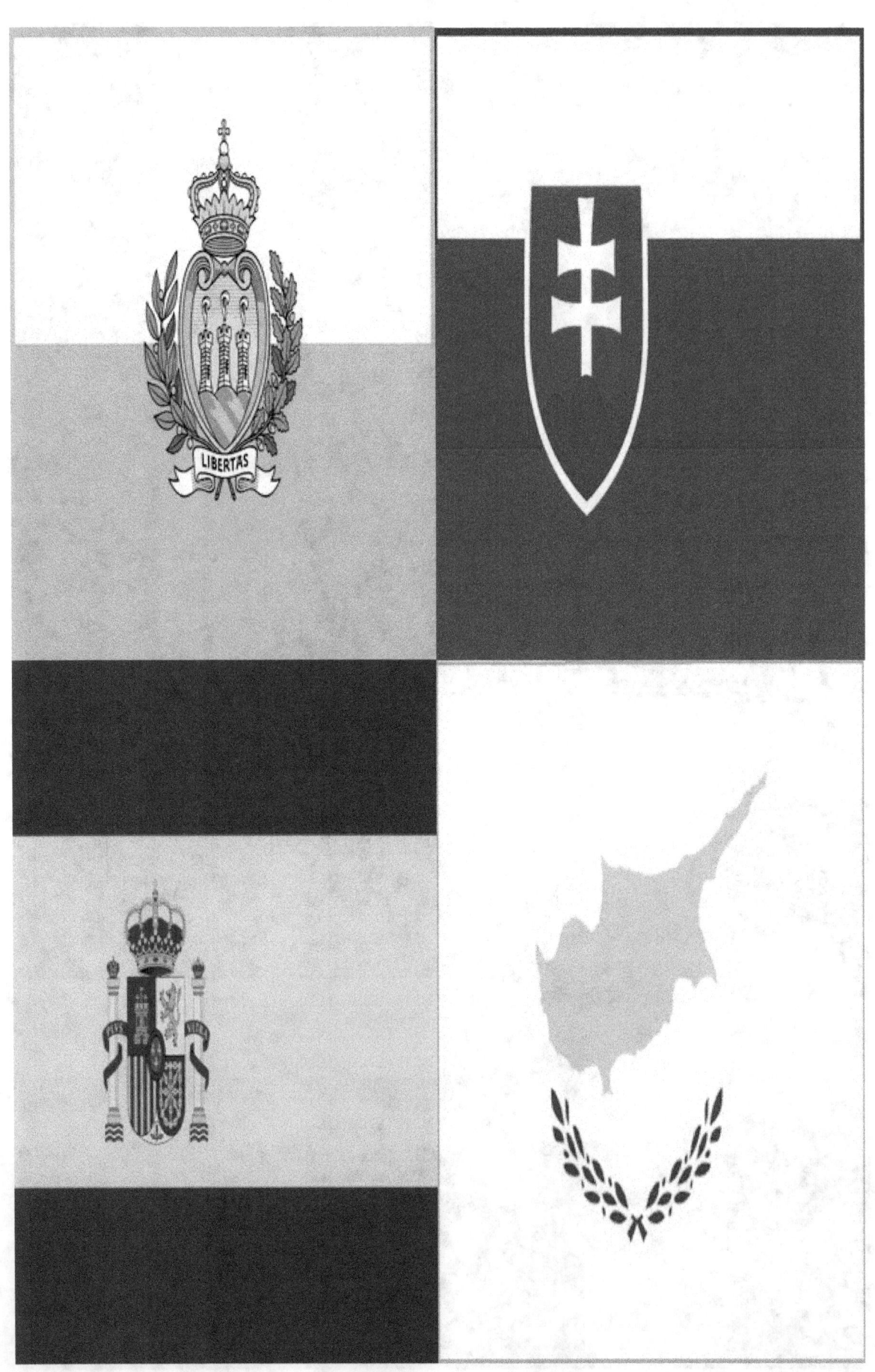

Arya Bàhram

Black Europe

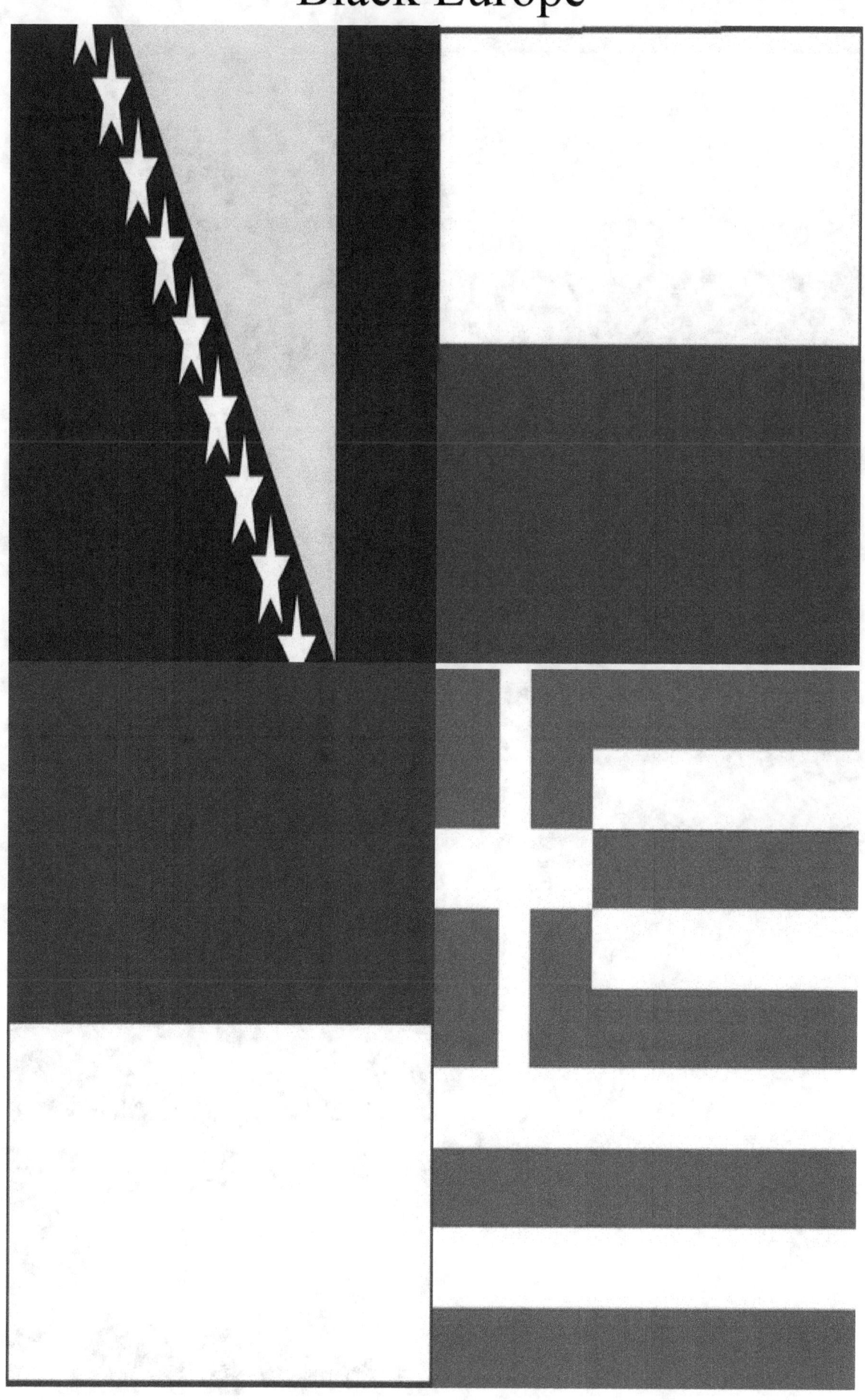

Arya Bàhram

Black Europe

Arya Bàhram

Black Europe

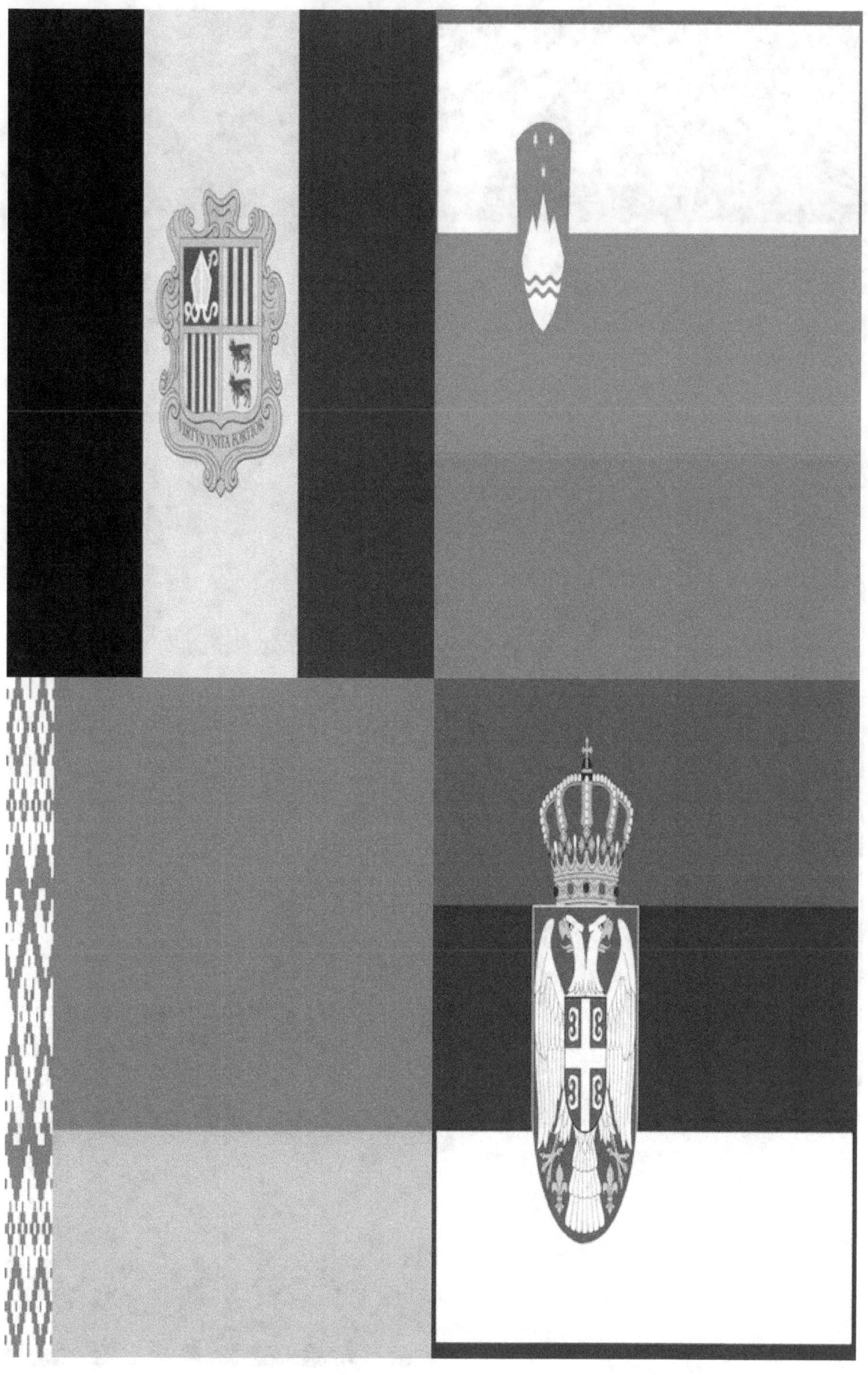

Arya Bàhram

Black Europe

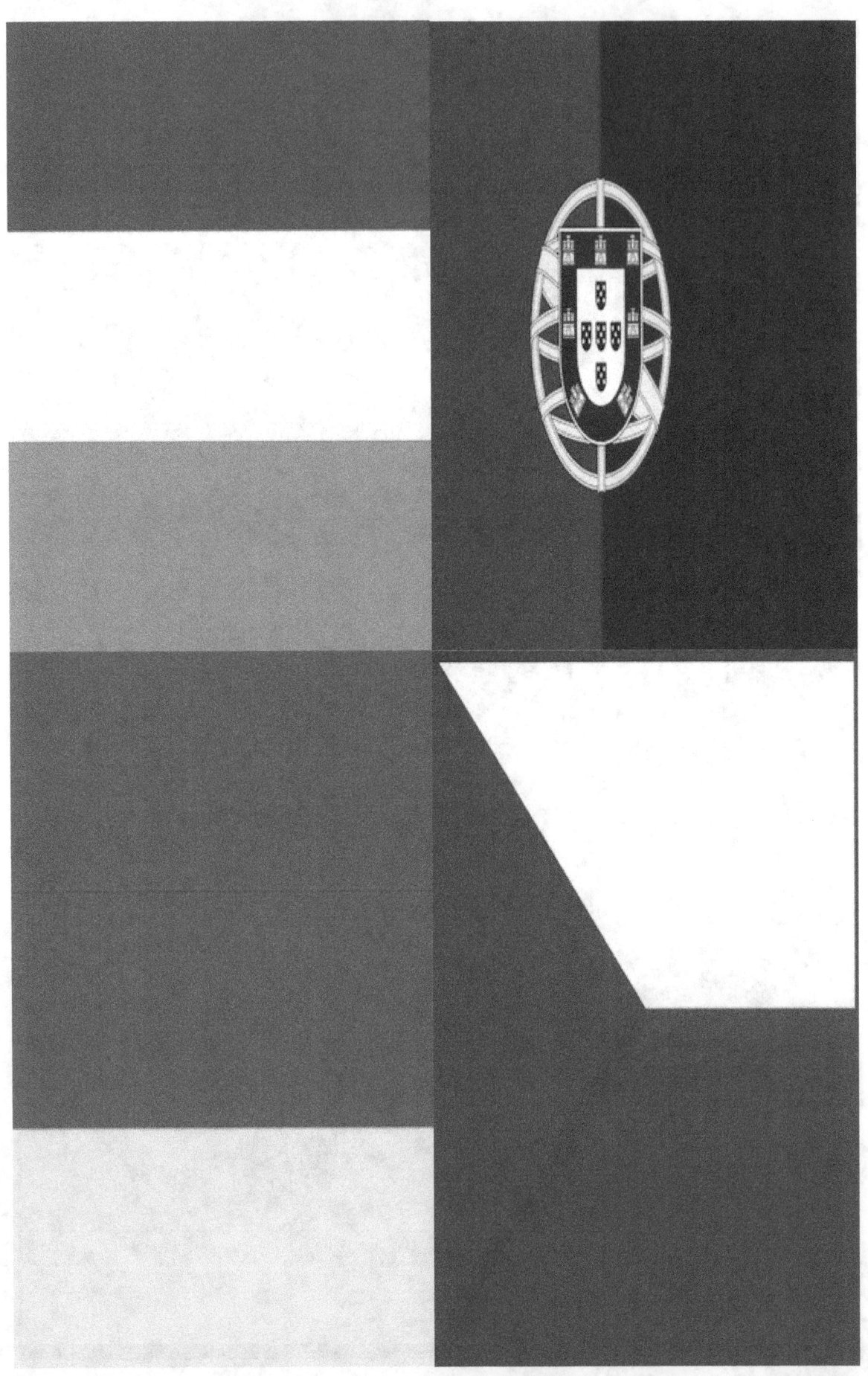

Arya Bàhram

Black Europe

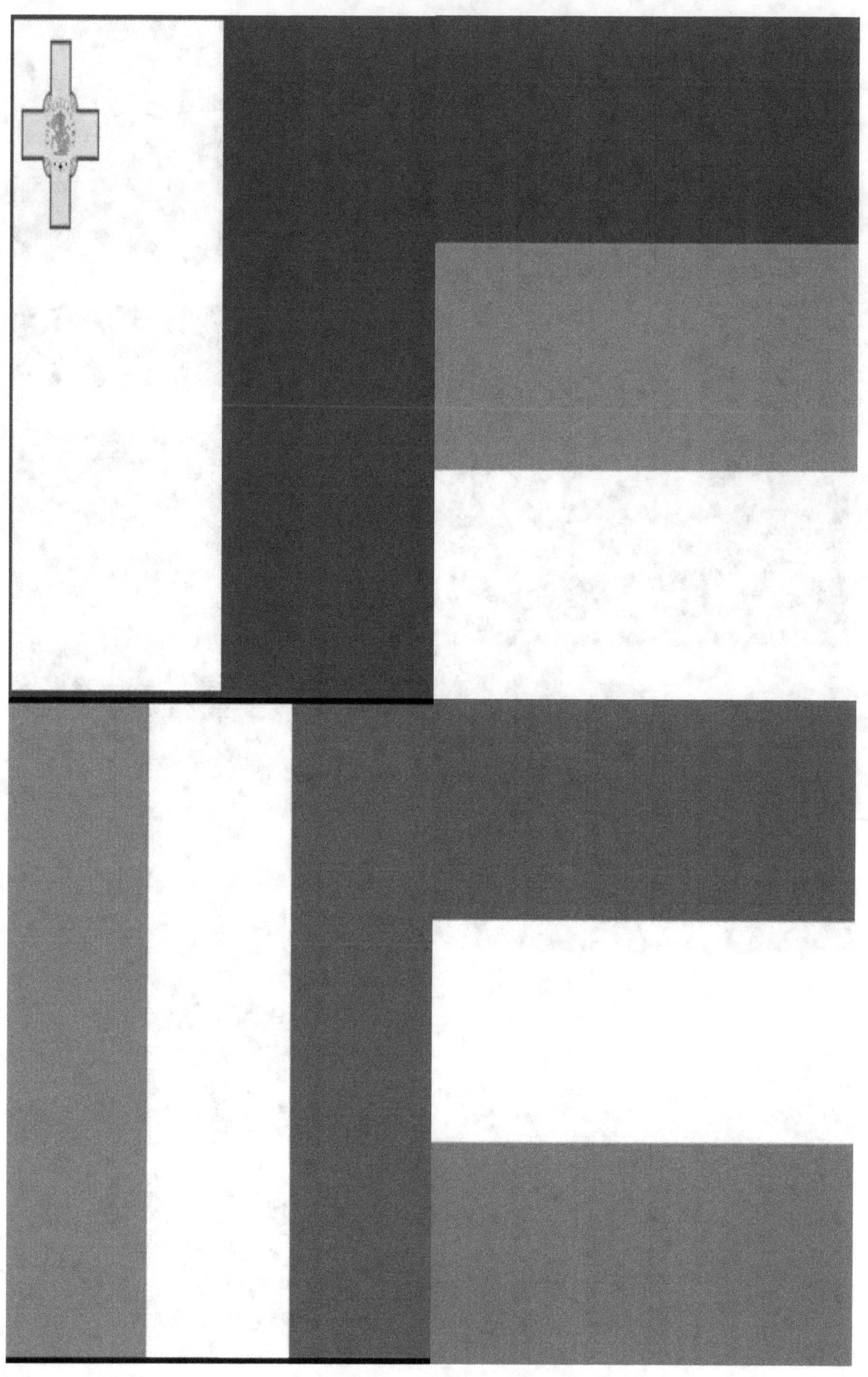

Arya Bàhram

Black Europe

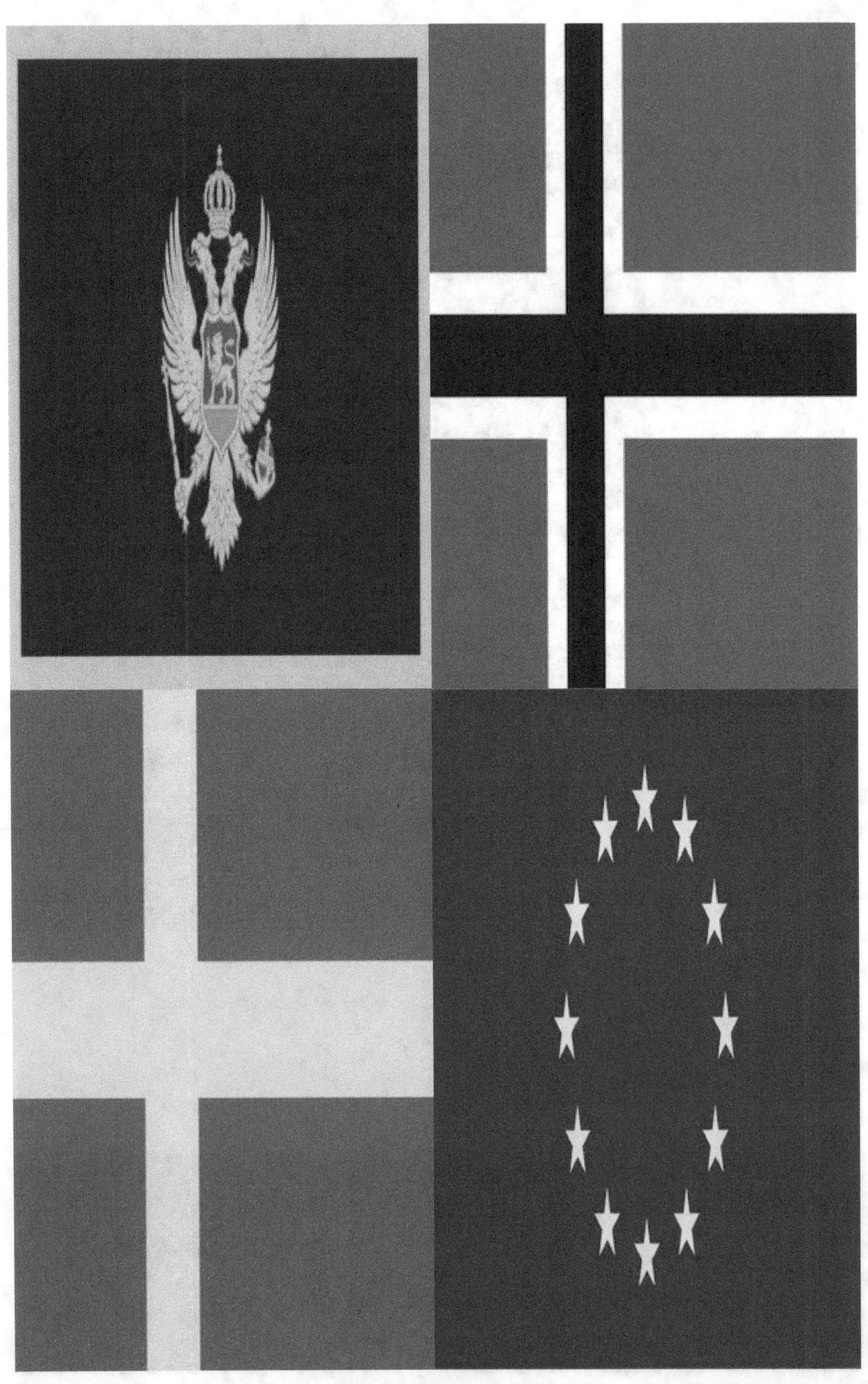

Arya Bàhram

Black Europe

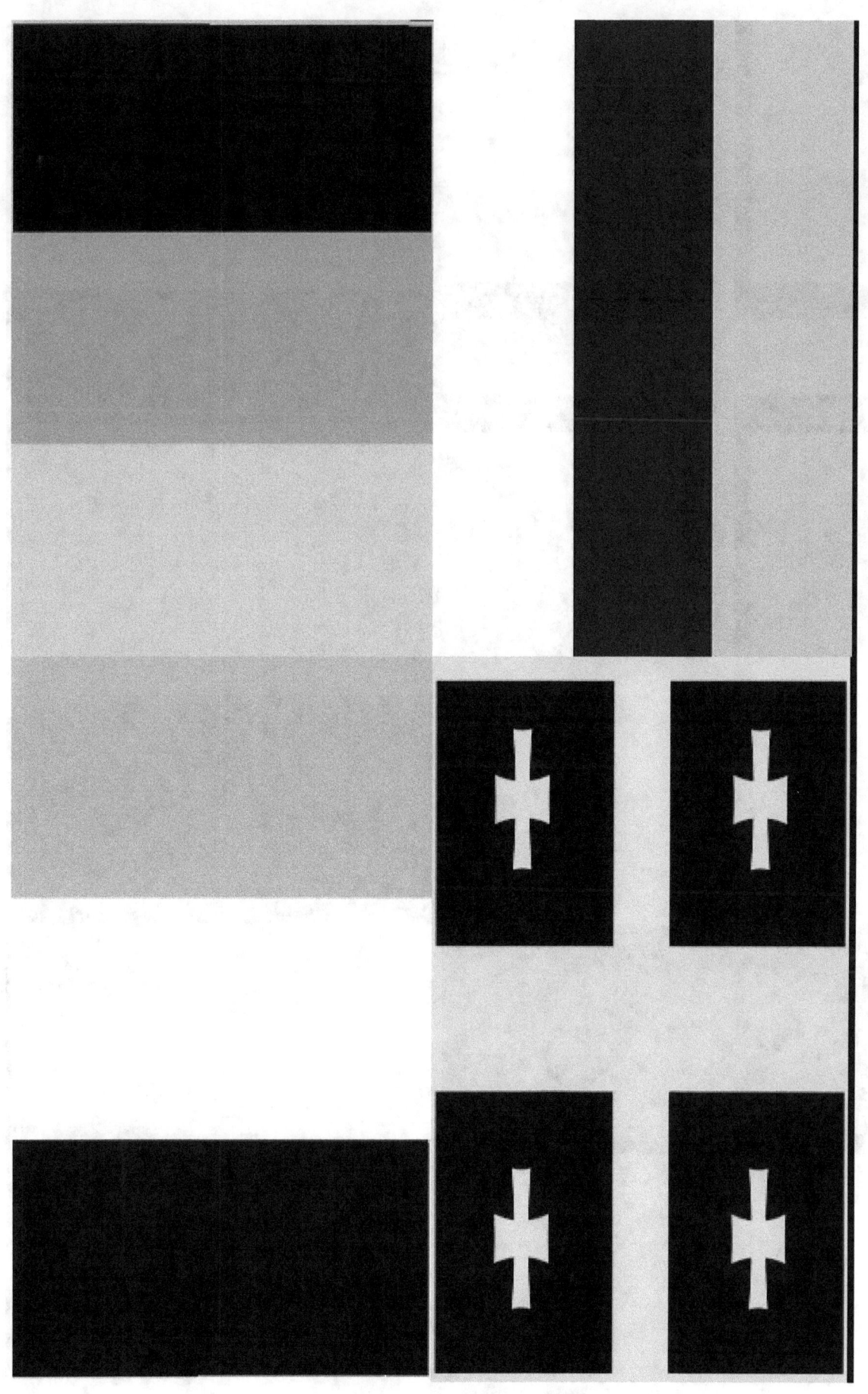

Arya Bàhram

Black Europe

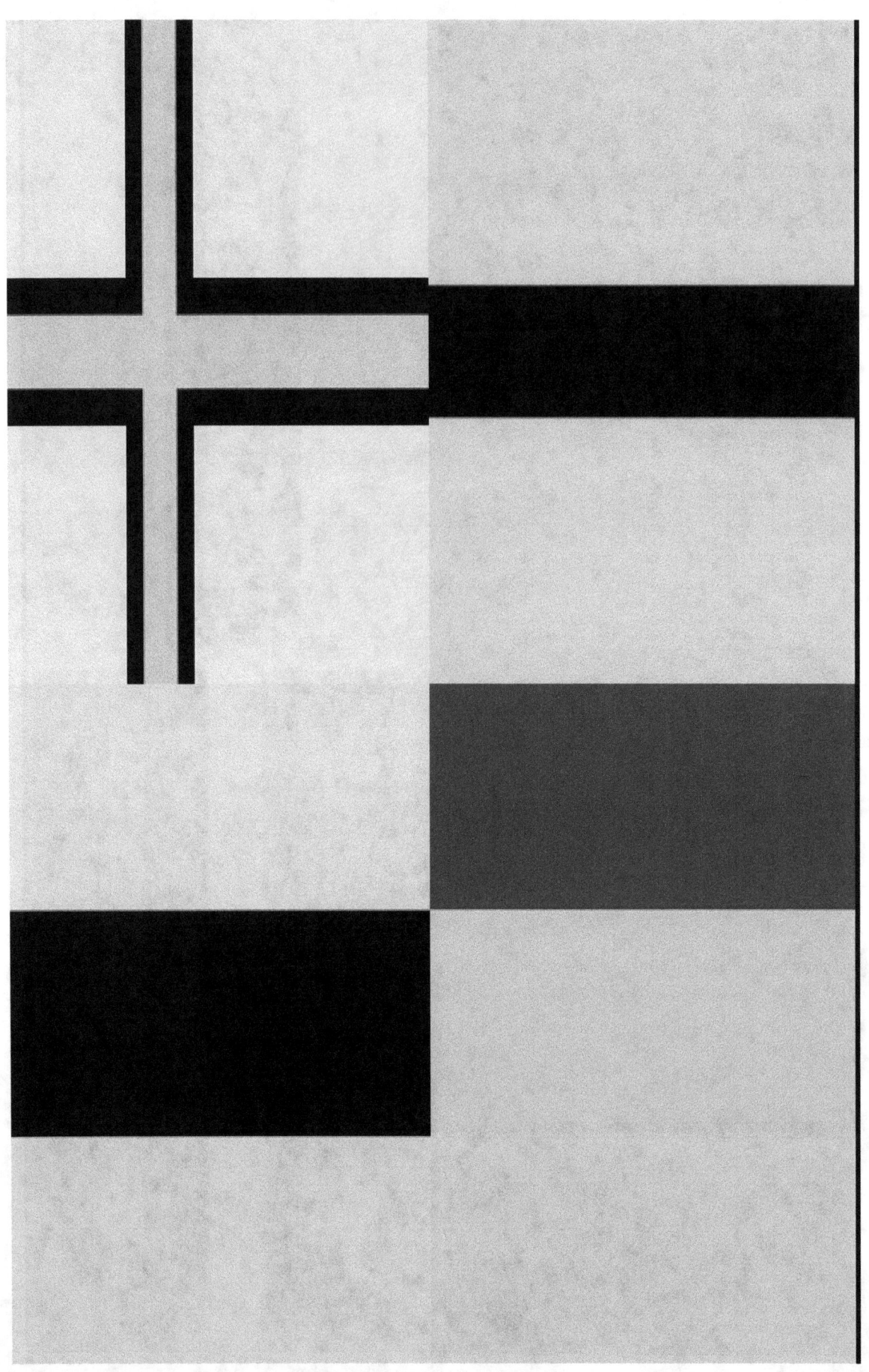

Arya Bàhram

Black Europe

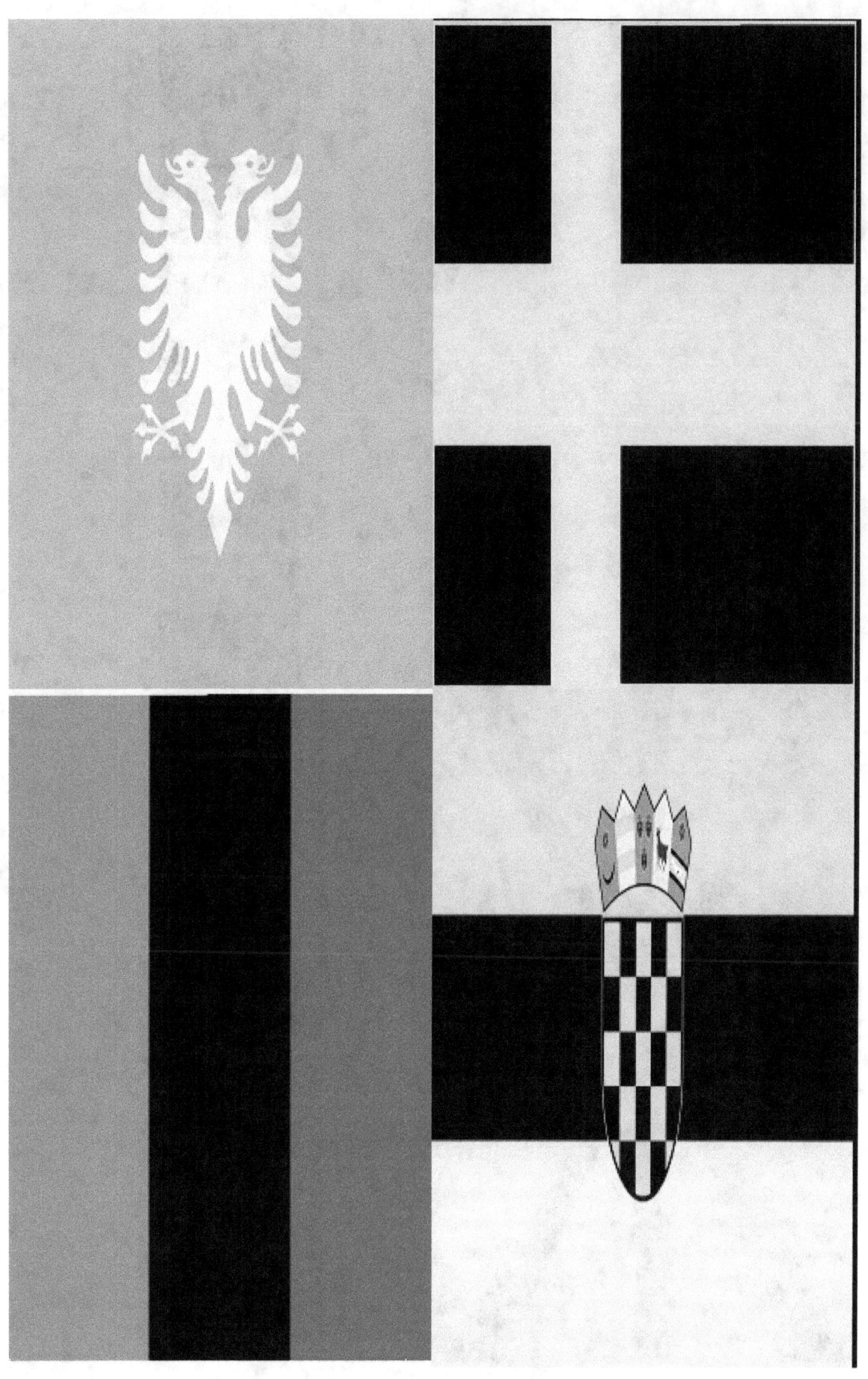

Arya Bàhram

Black Europe

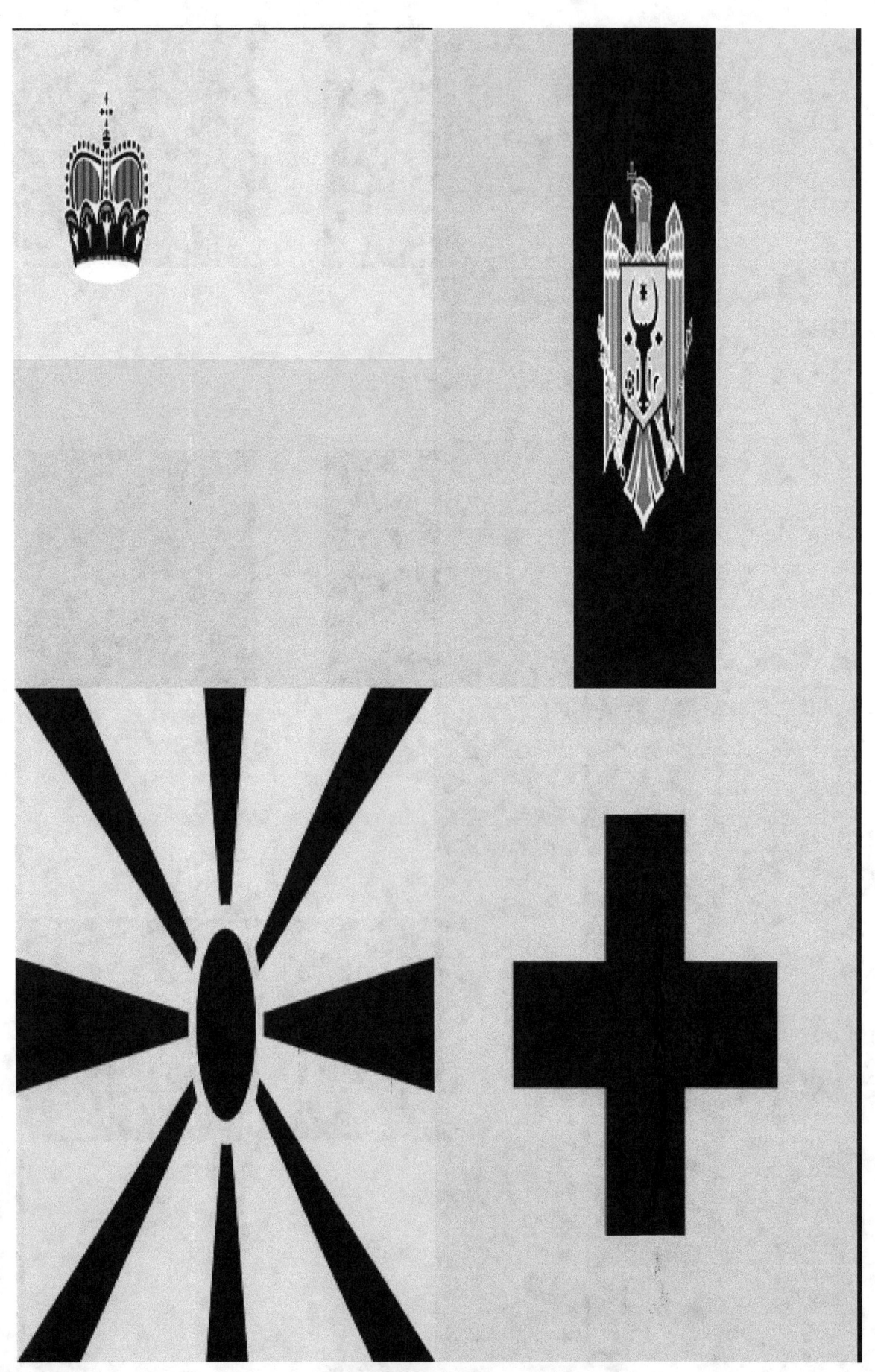

Arya Bàhram

Black Europe

Arya Bàhram

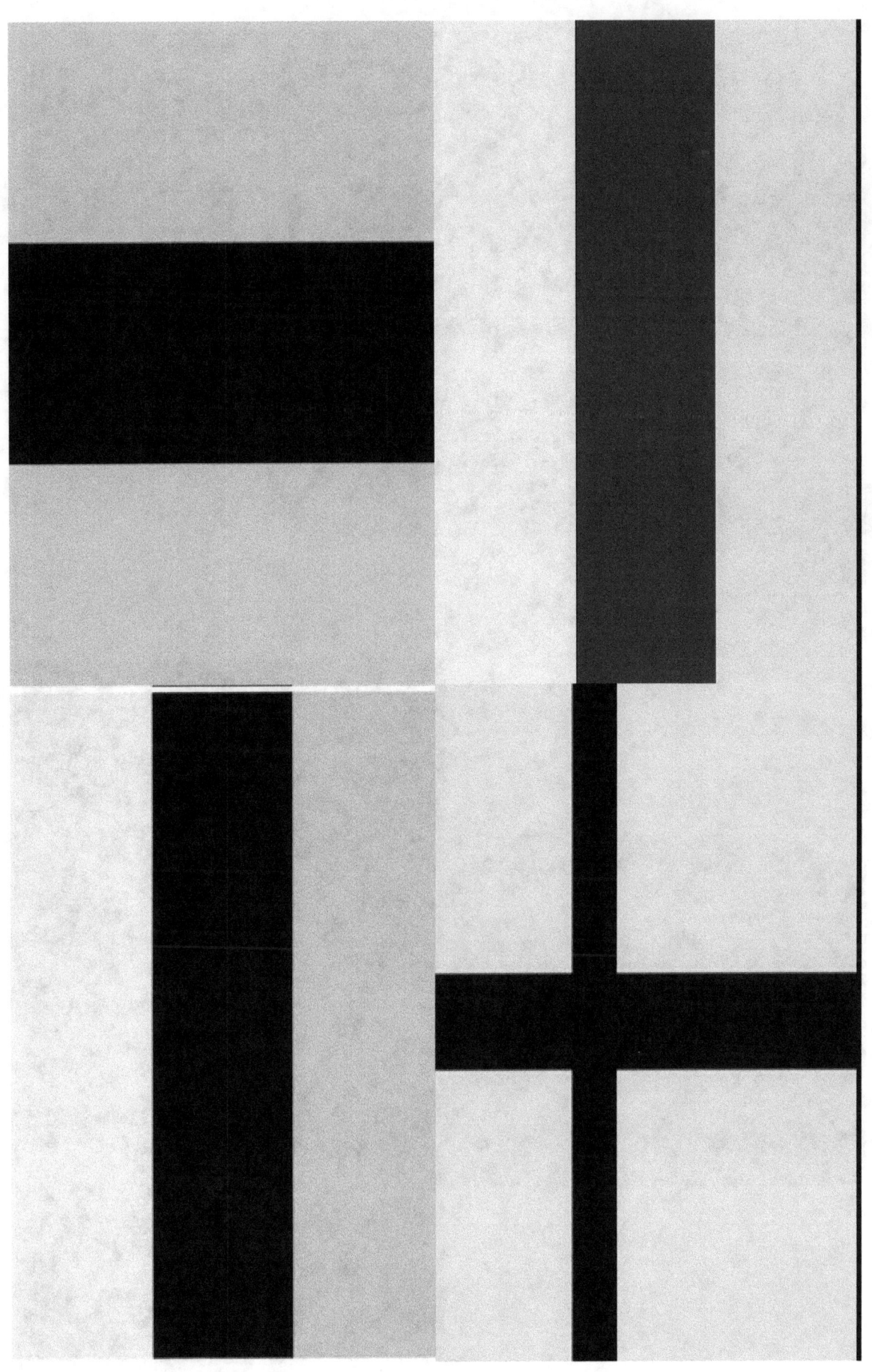

Black Europe

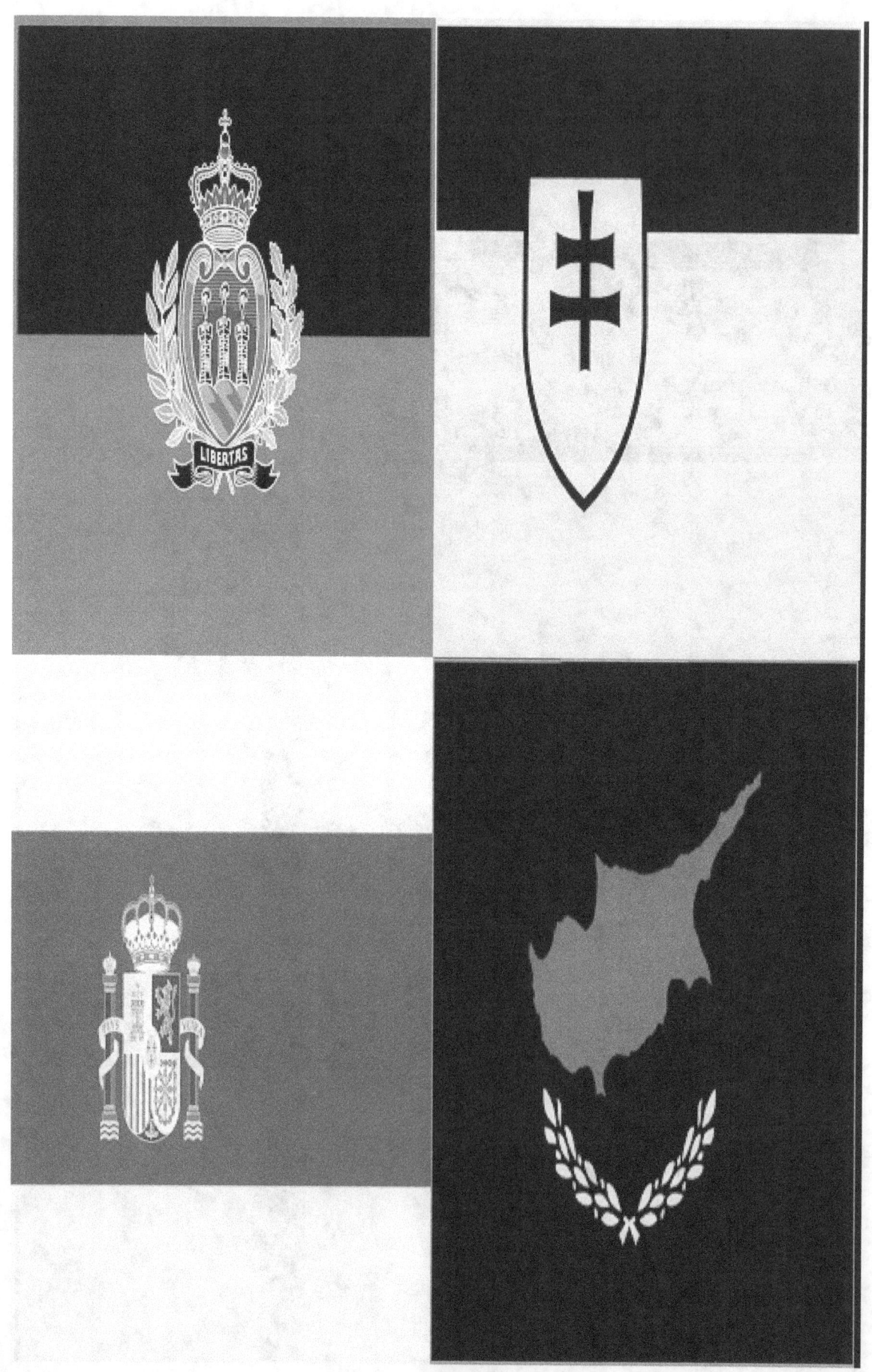

Arya Bàhram

Black Europe

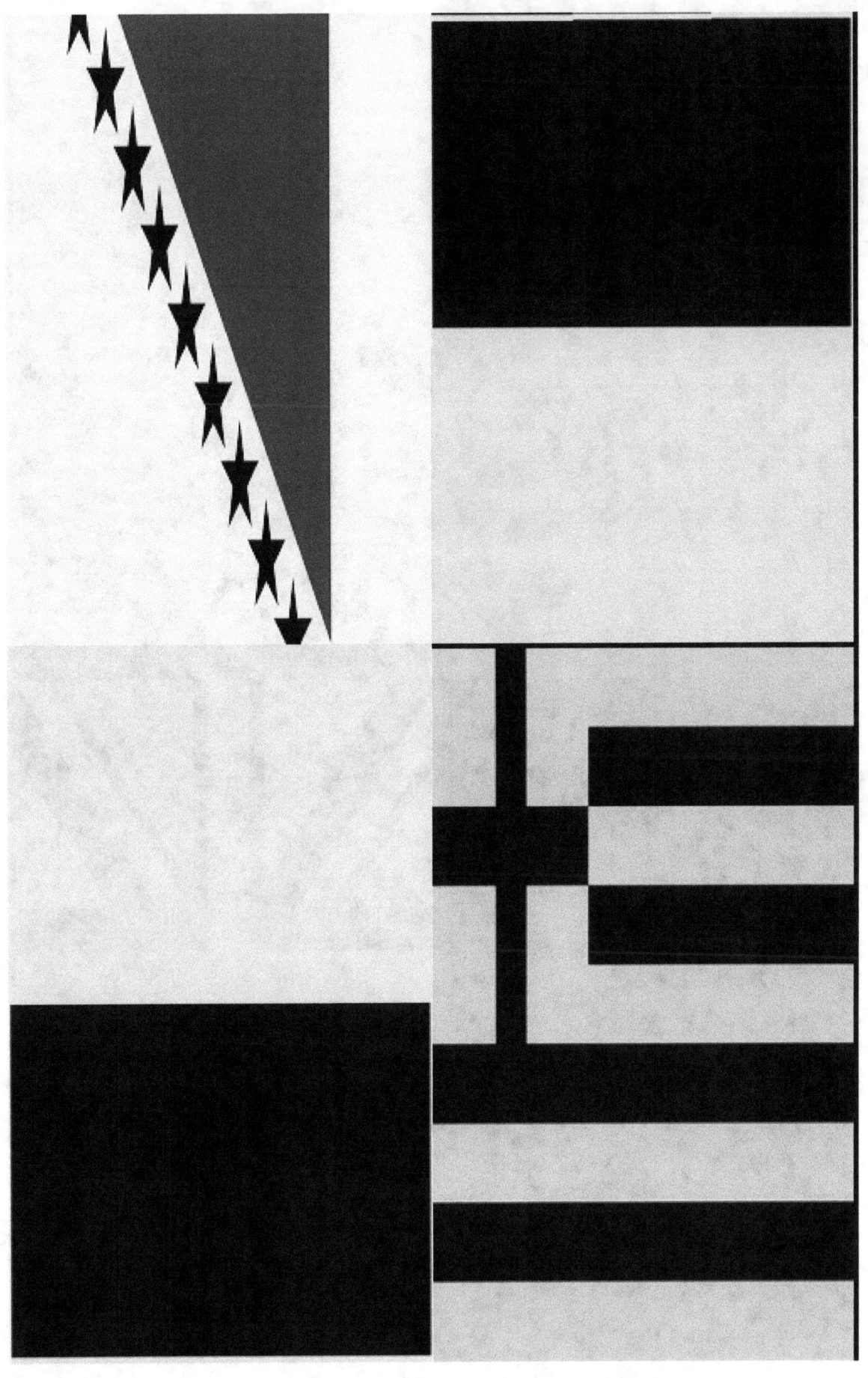

Arya Bàhram

Black Europe

Arya Bàhram

Black Europe

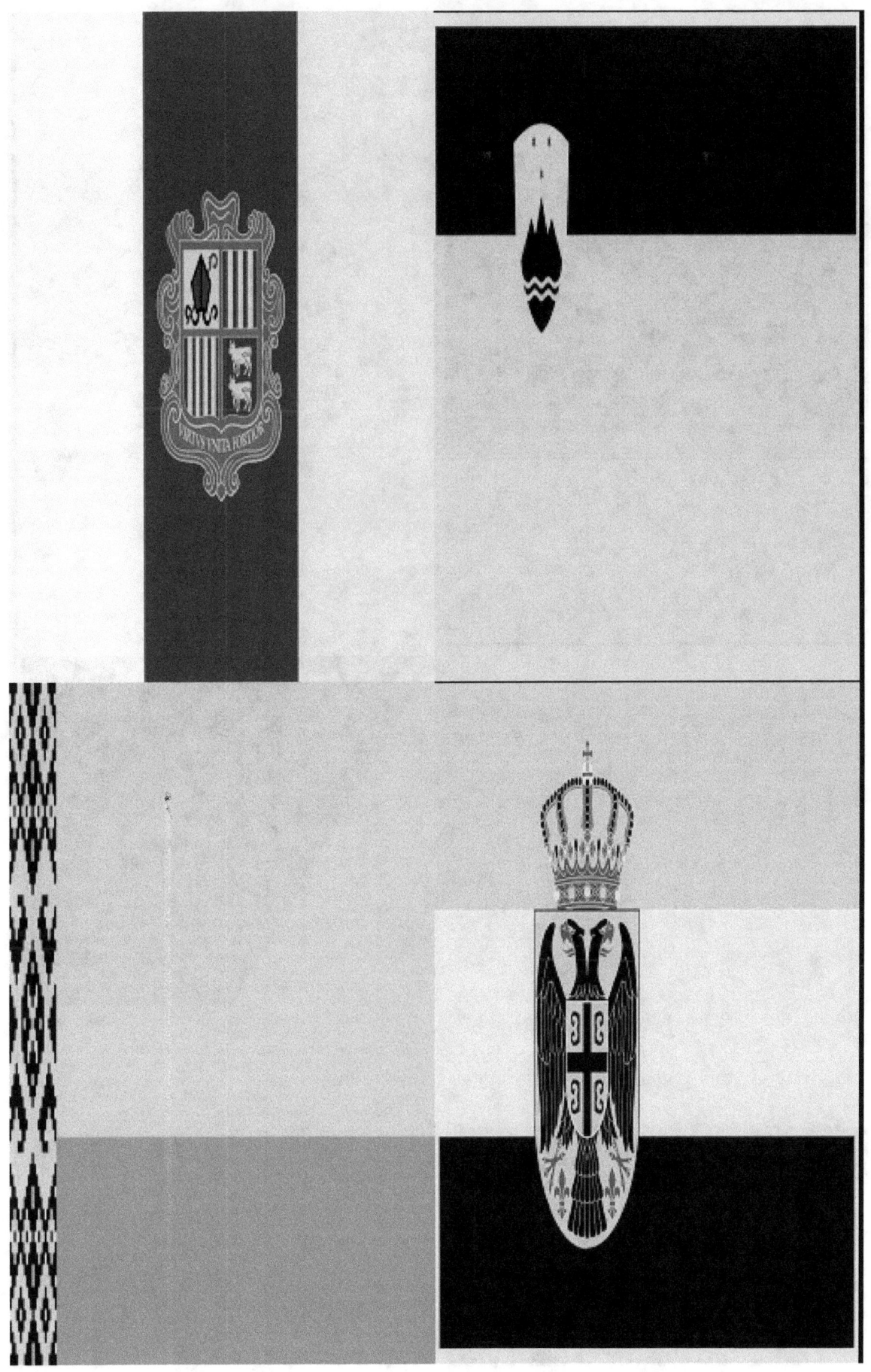

Arya Bàhram

Black Europe

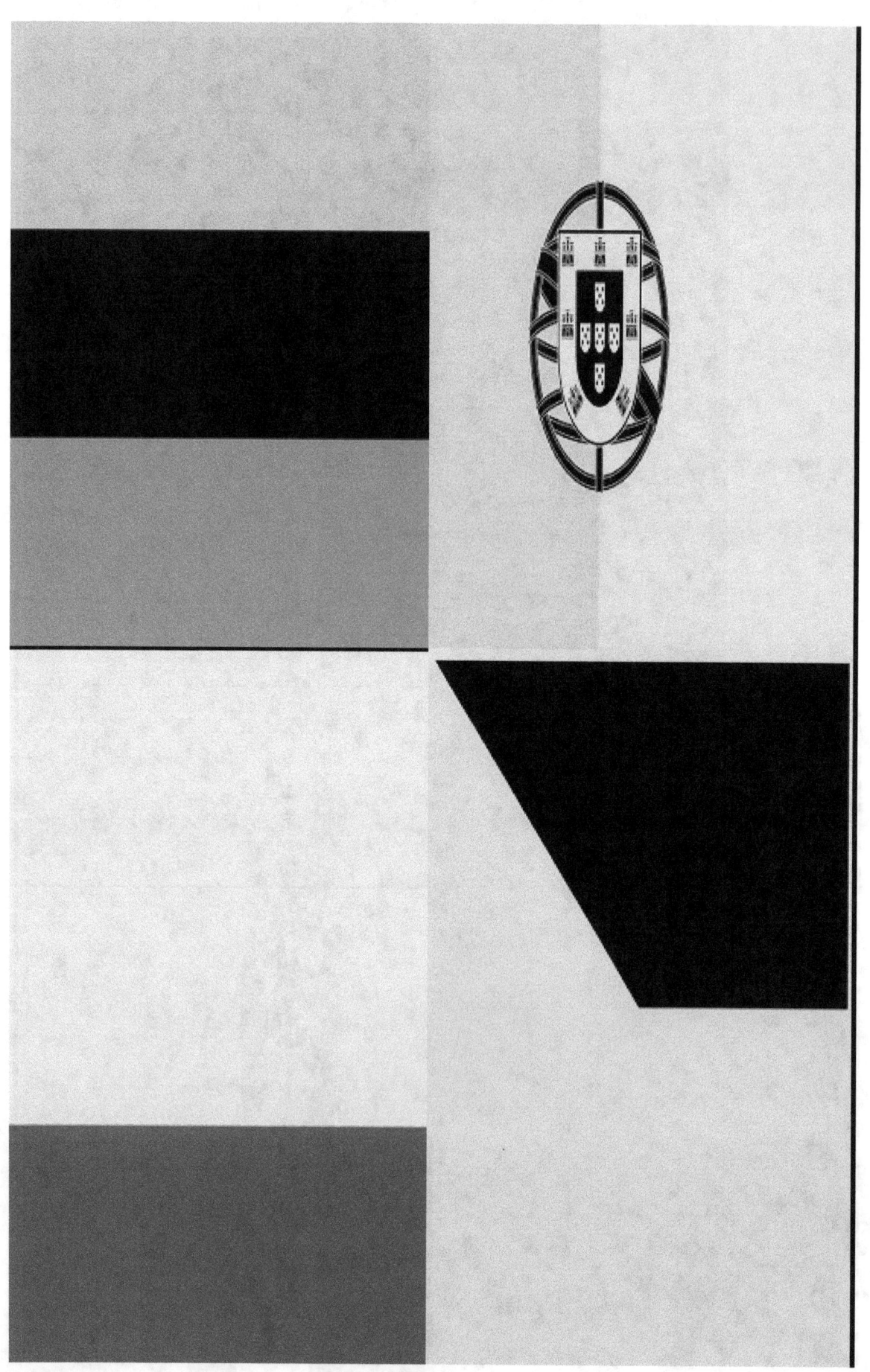

Arya Bàhram

Black Europe

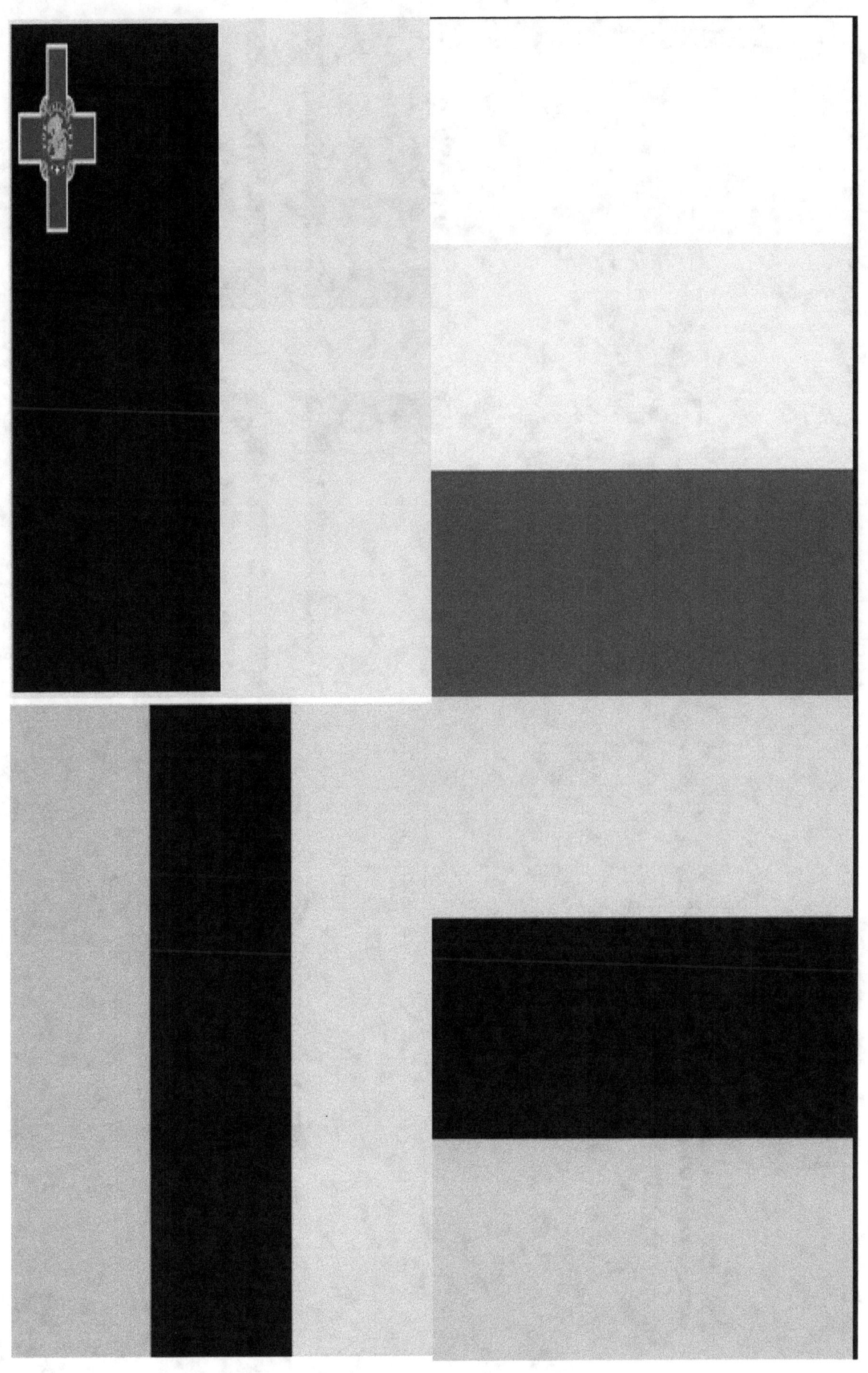

Arya Bàhram

Black Europe

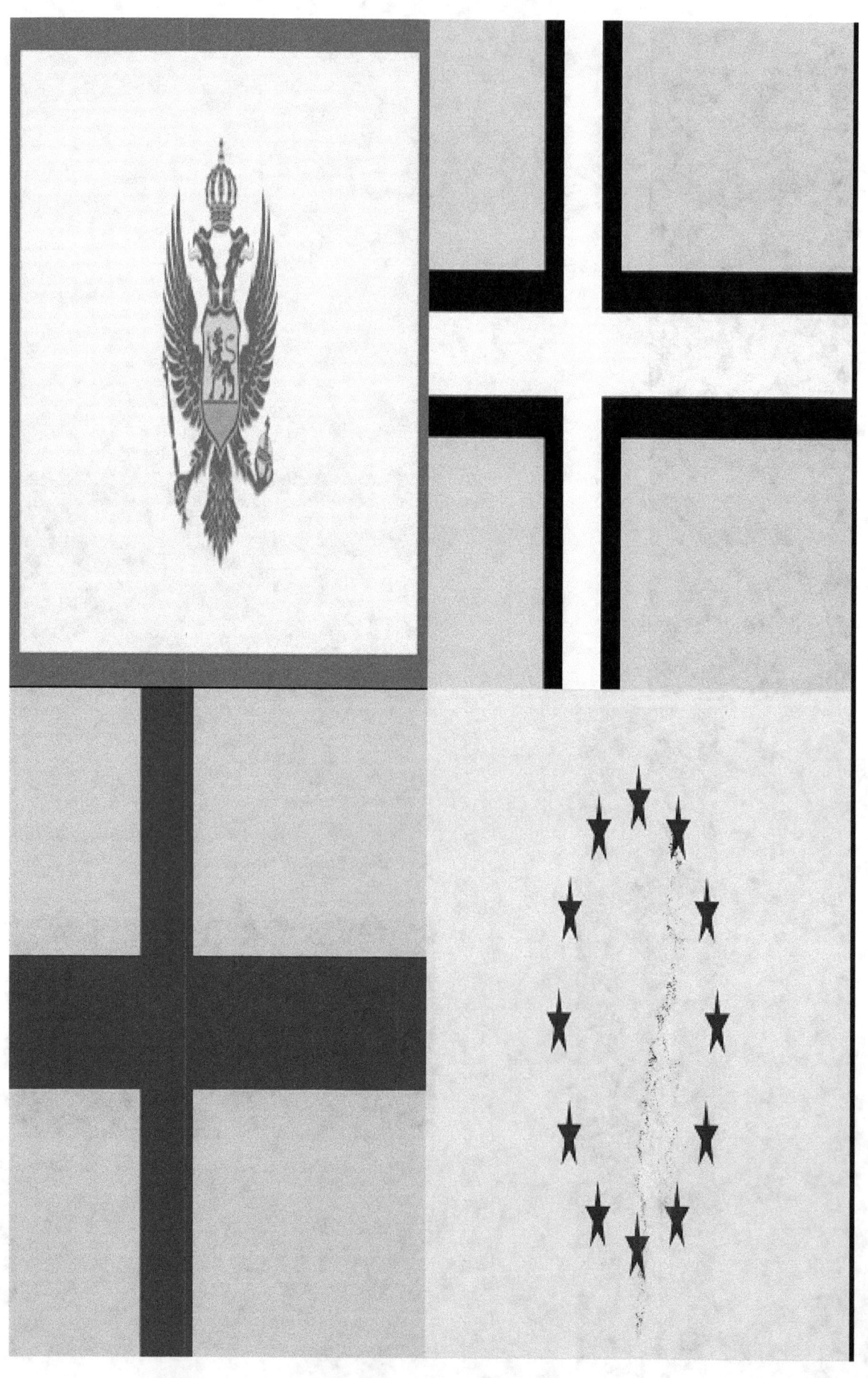

Arya Bàhram

Black Europe

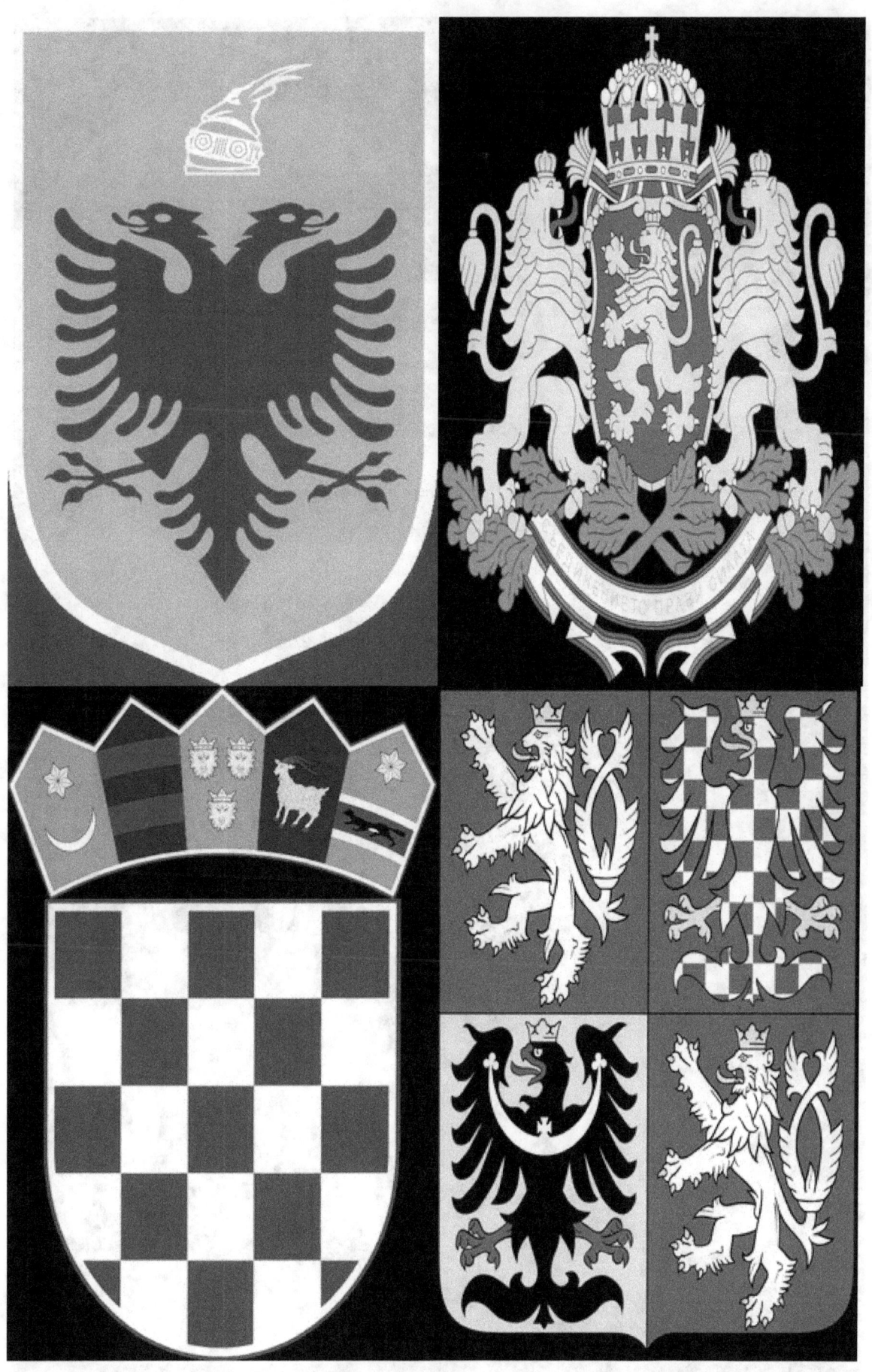

Arya Bàhram

Black Europe

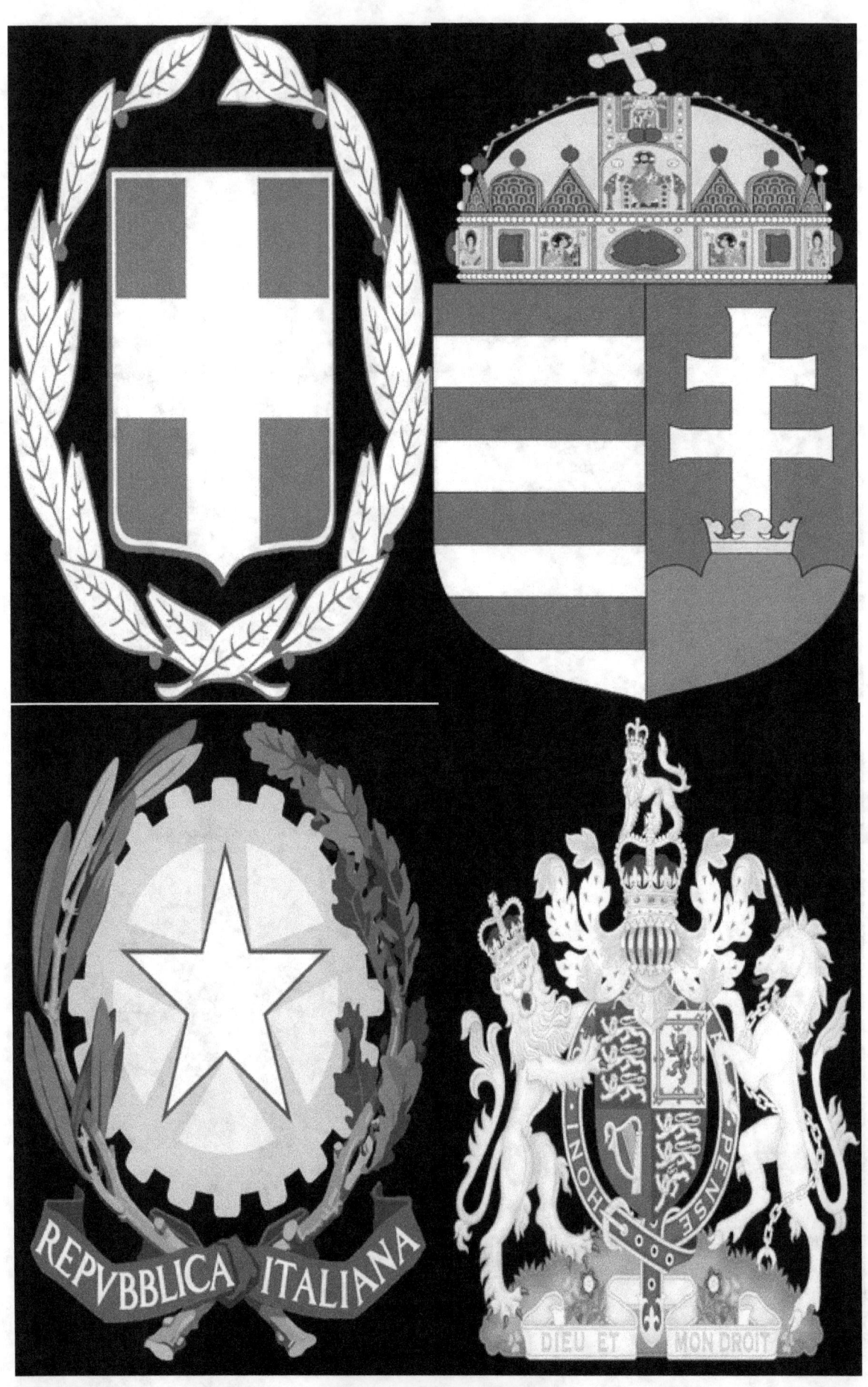

Arya Bàhram

Black Europe

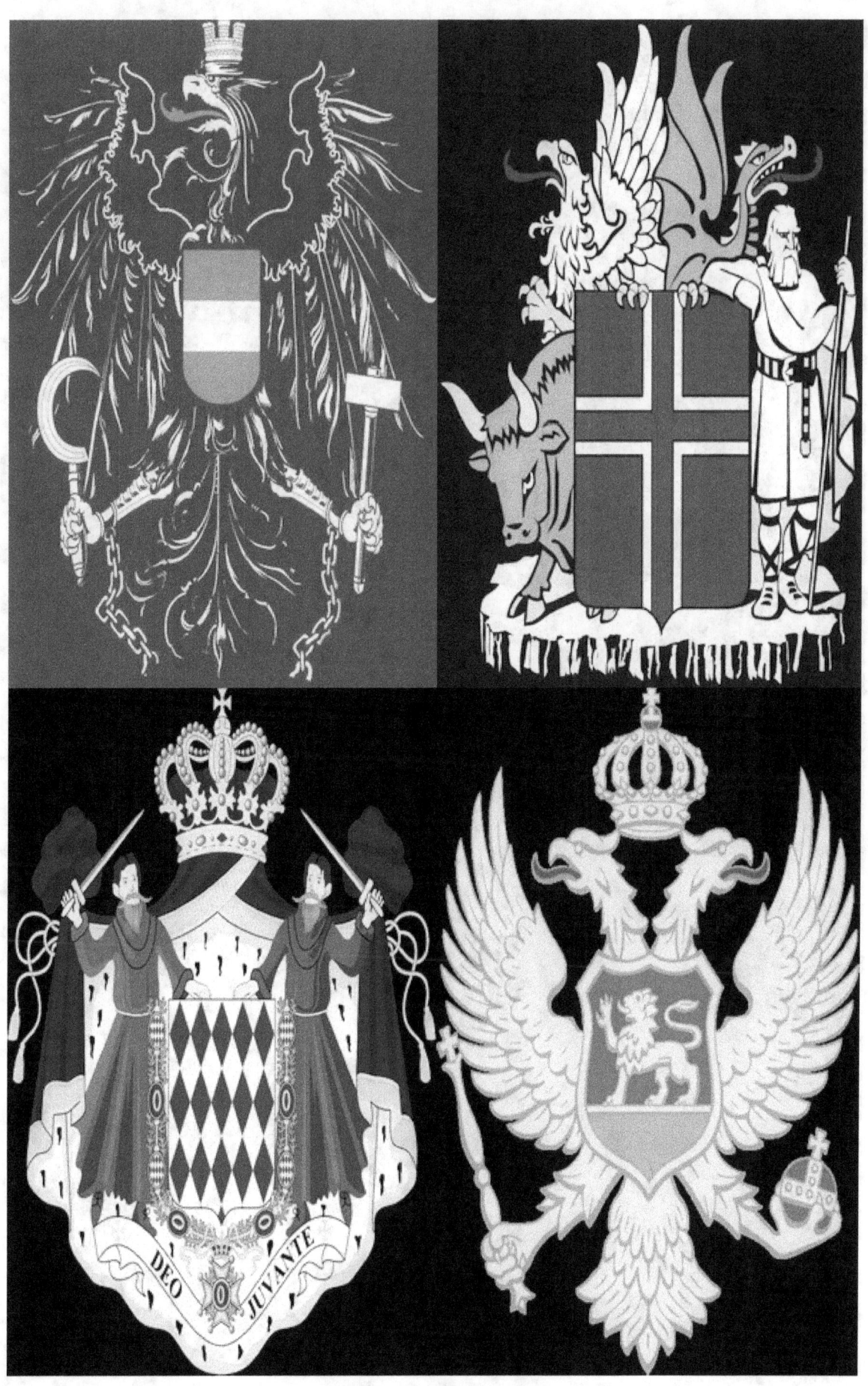

Arya Bàhram

Black Europe

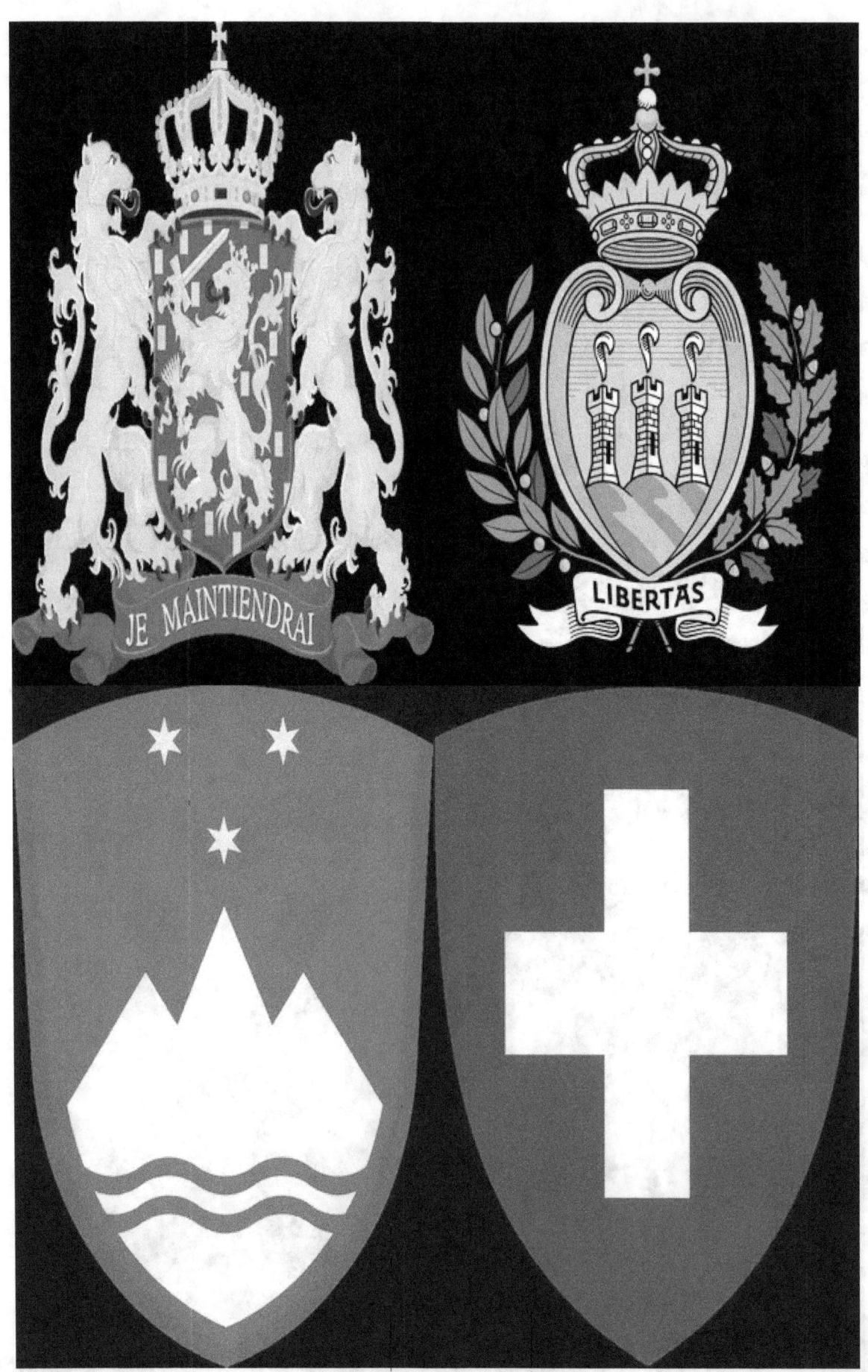

Arya Bàhram

Black Europe

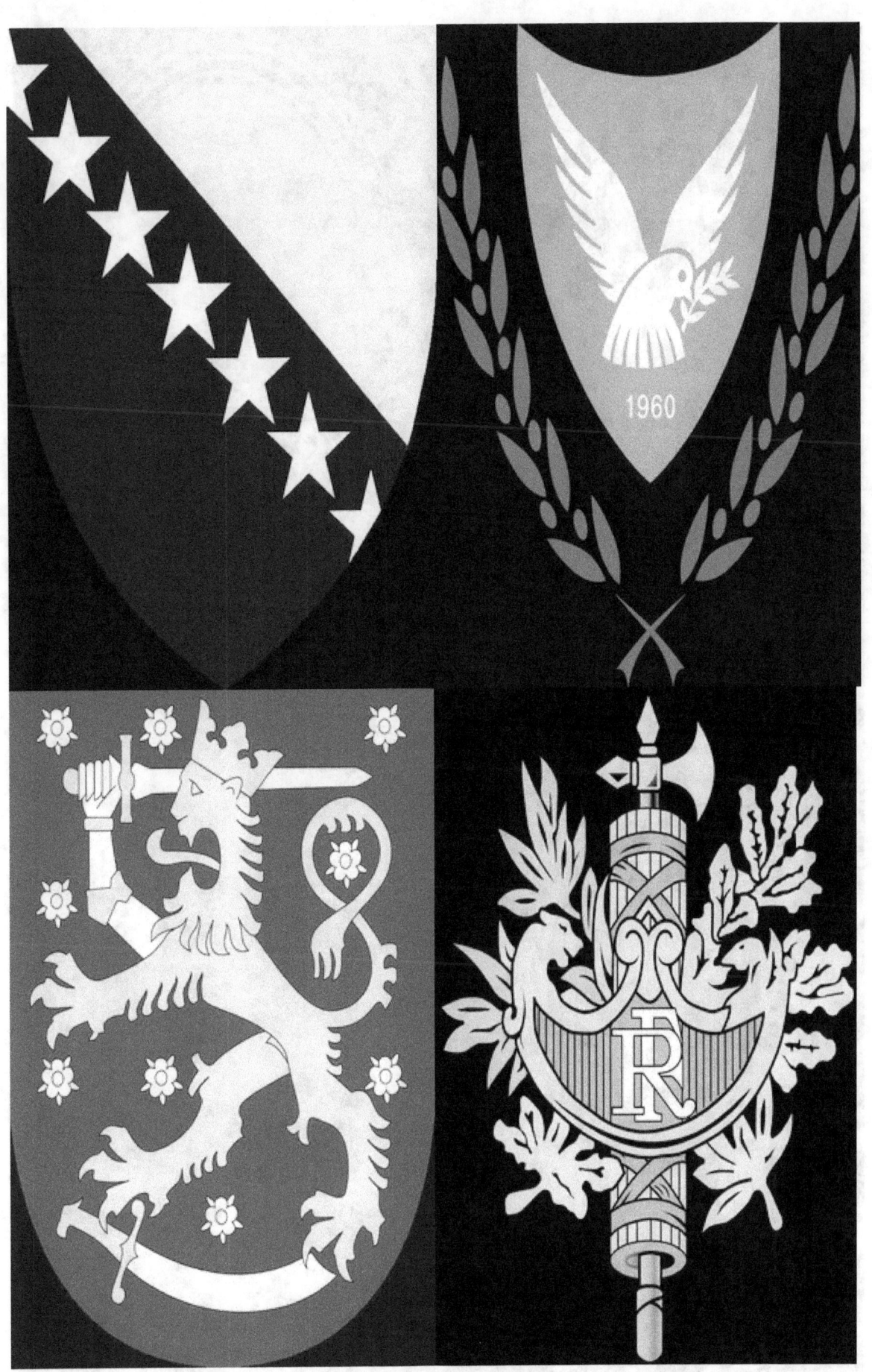

Arya Bàhram

Black Europe

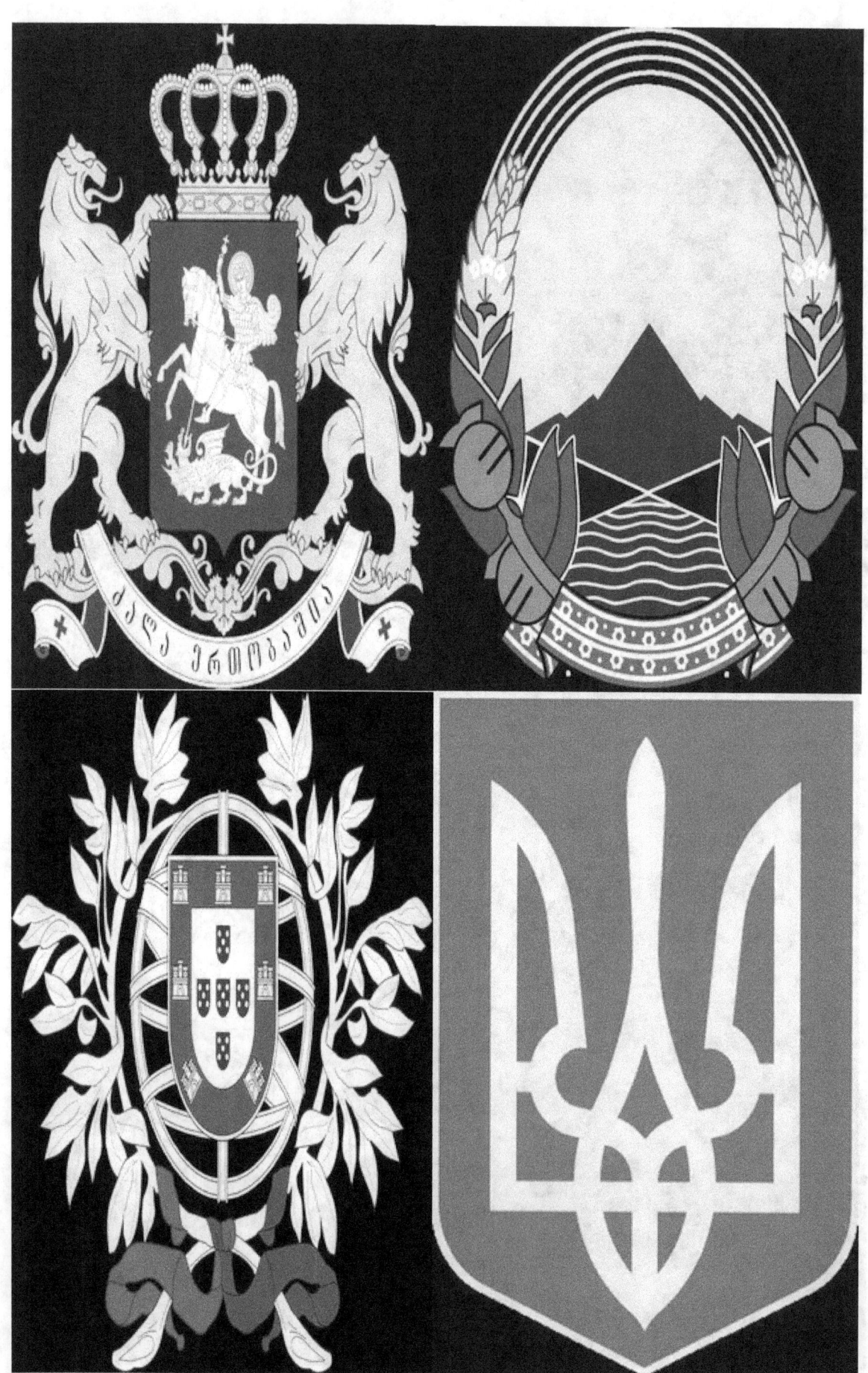

Arya Bàhram

Black Europe

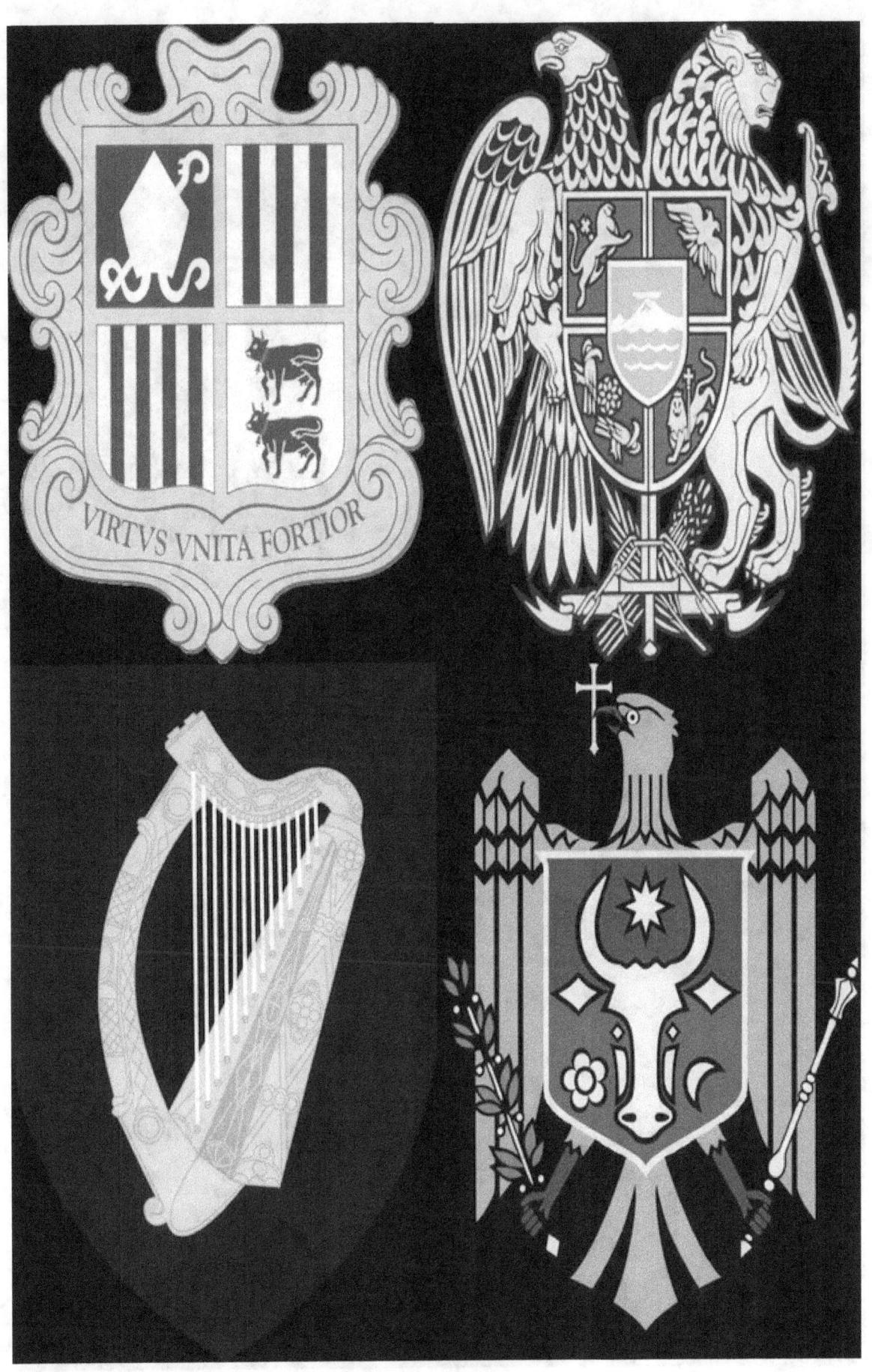

VIRTVS VNITA FORTIOR

Arya Bàhram

Black Europe

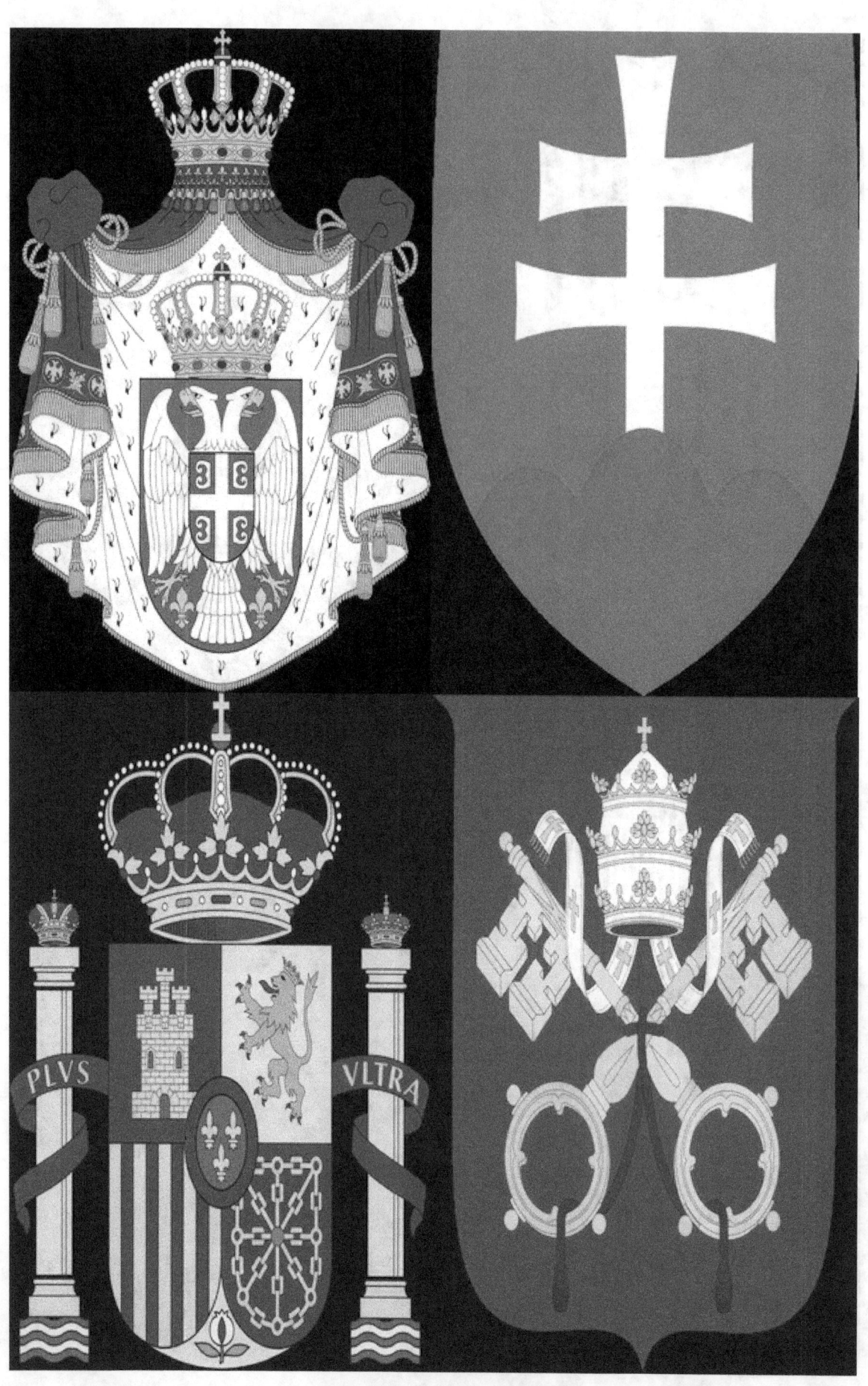

Arya Bàhram

Black Europe

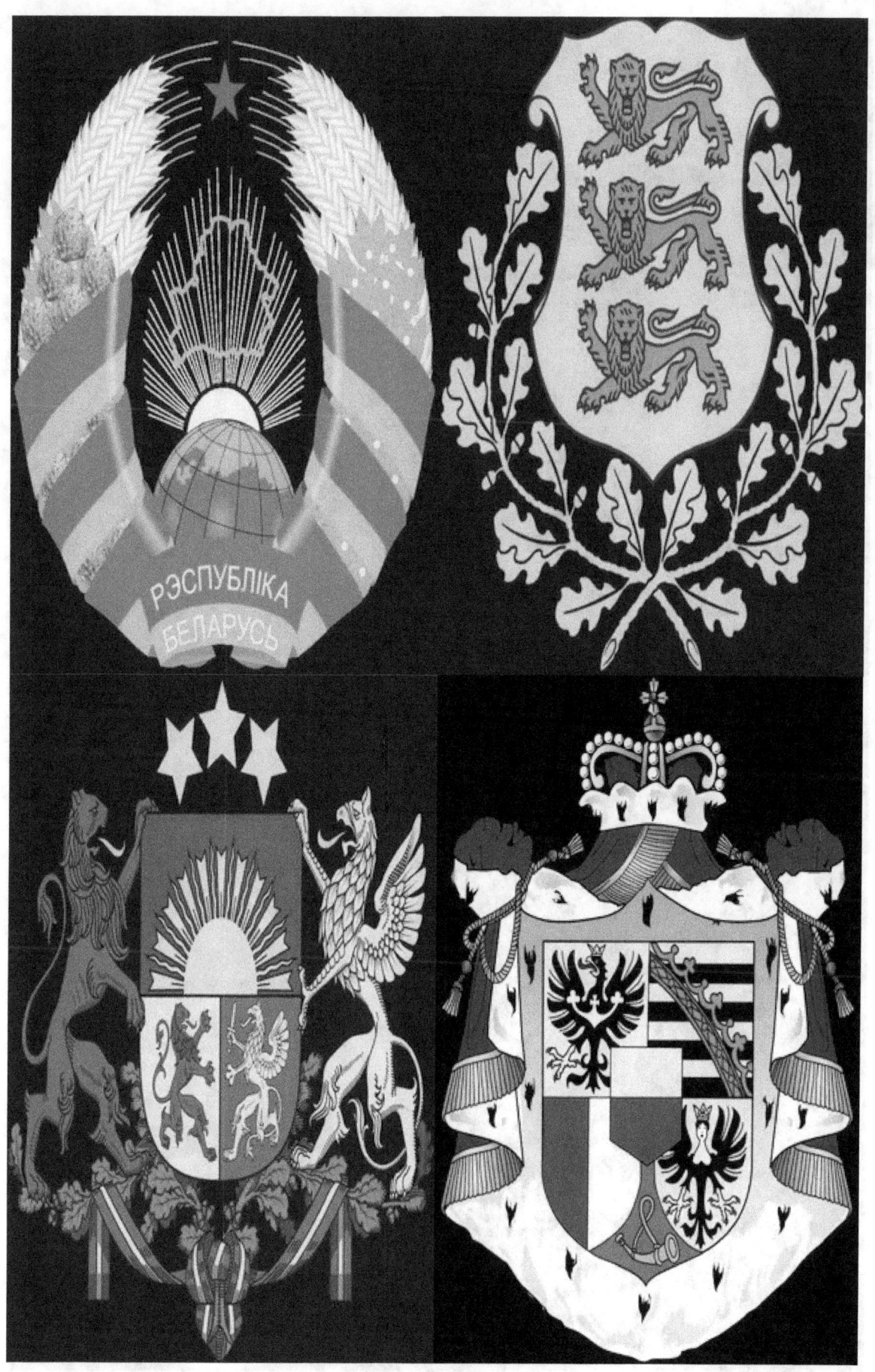

Arya Bàhram

Black Europe

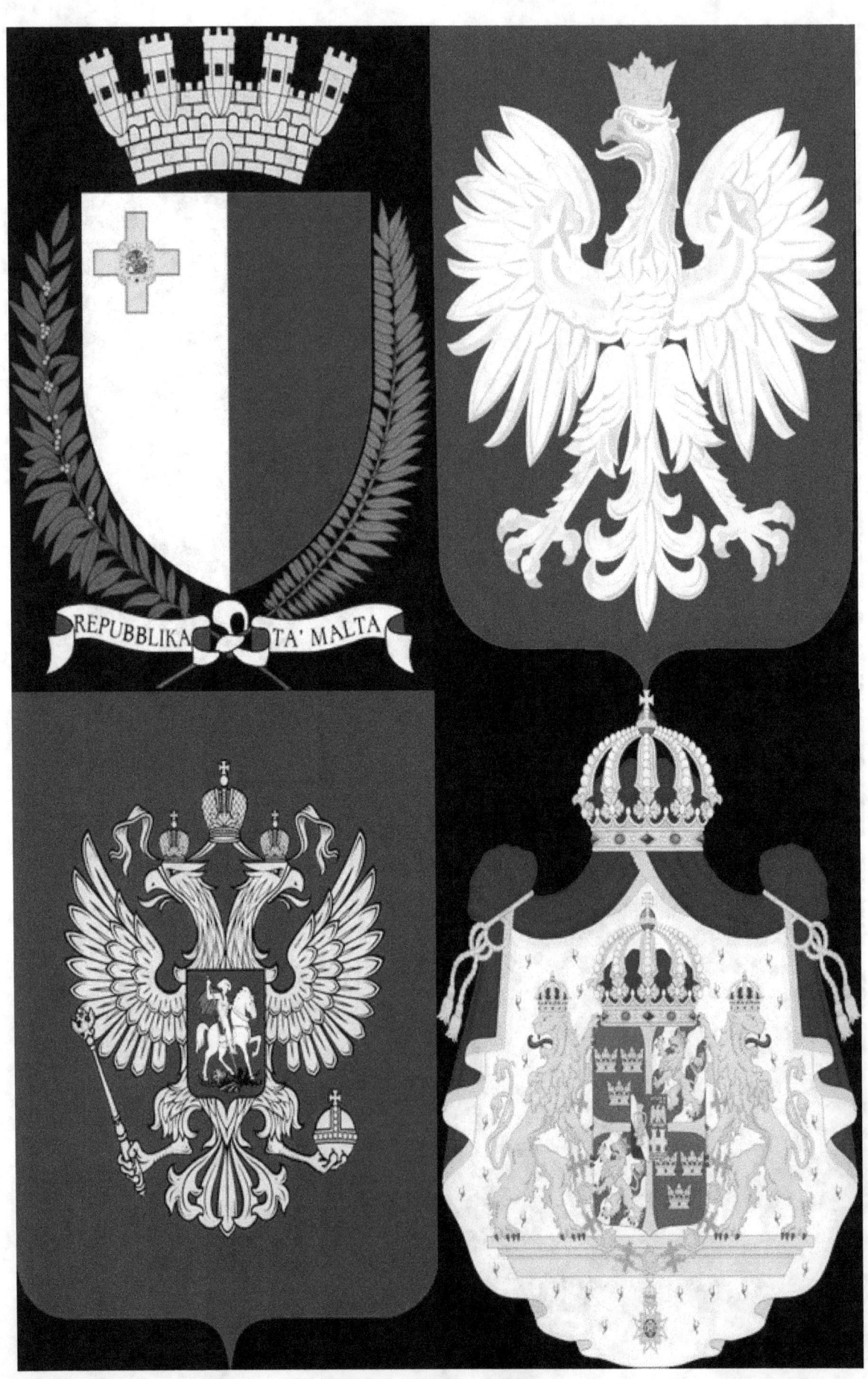

Arya Bàhram

Black Europe

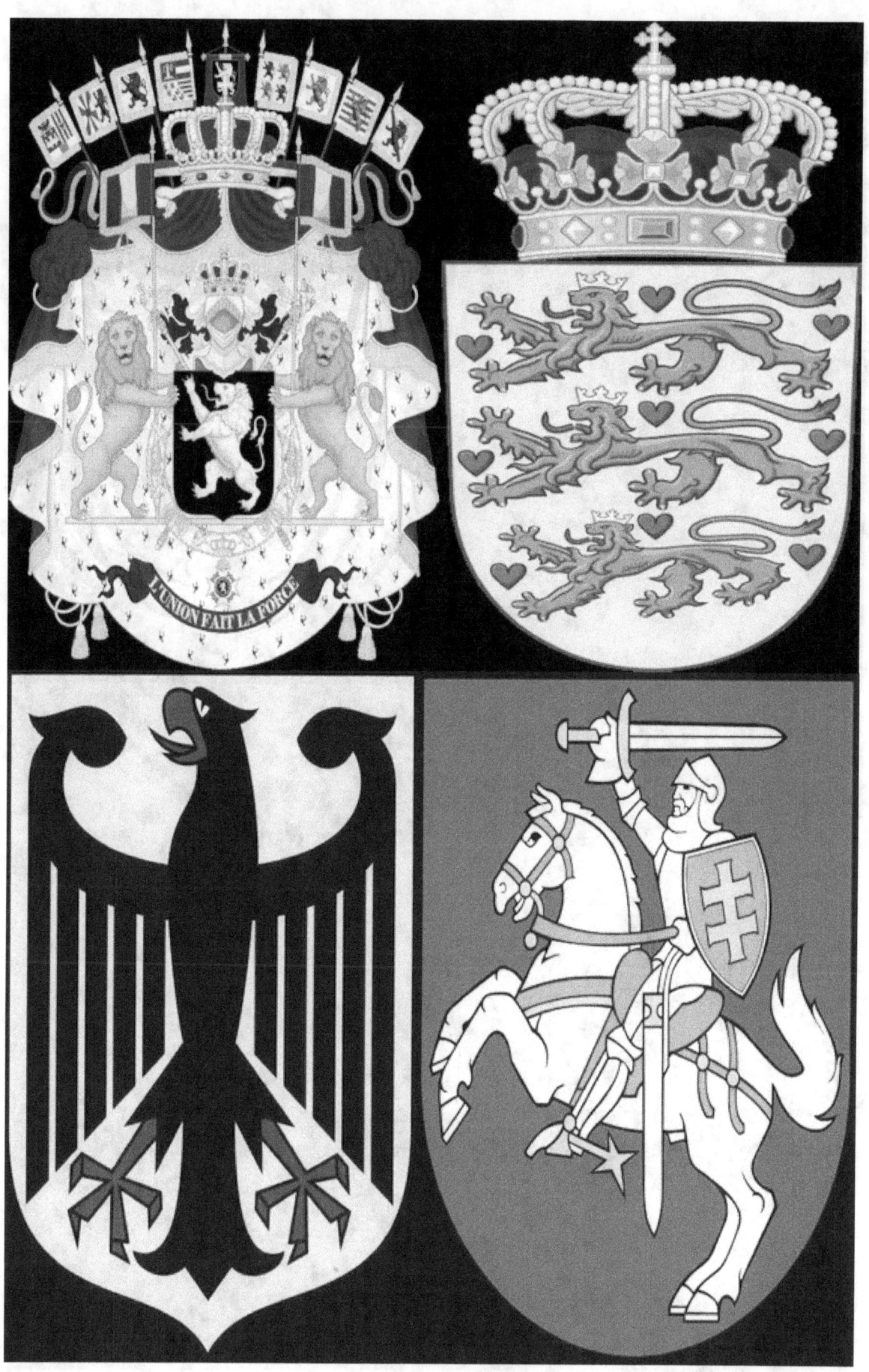

Arya Bàhram

Black Europe

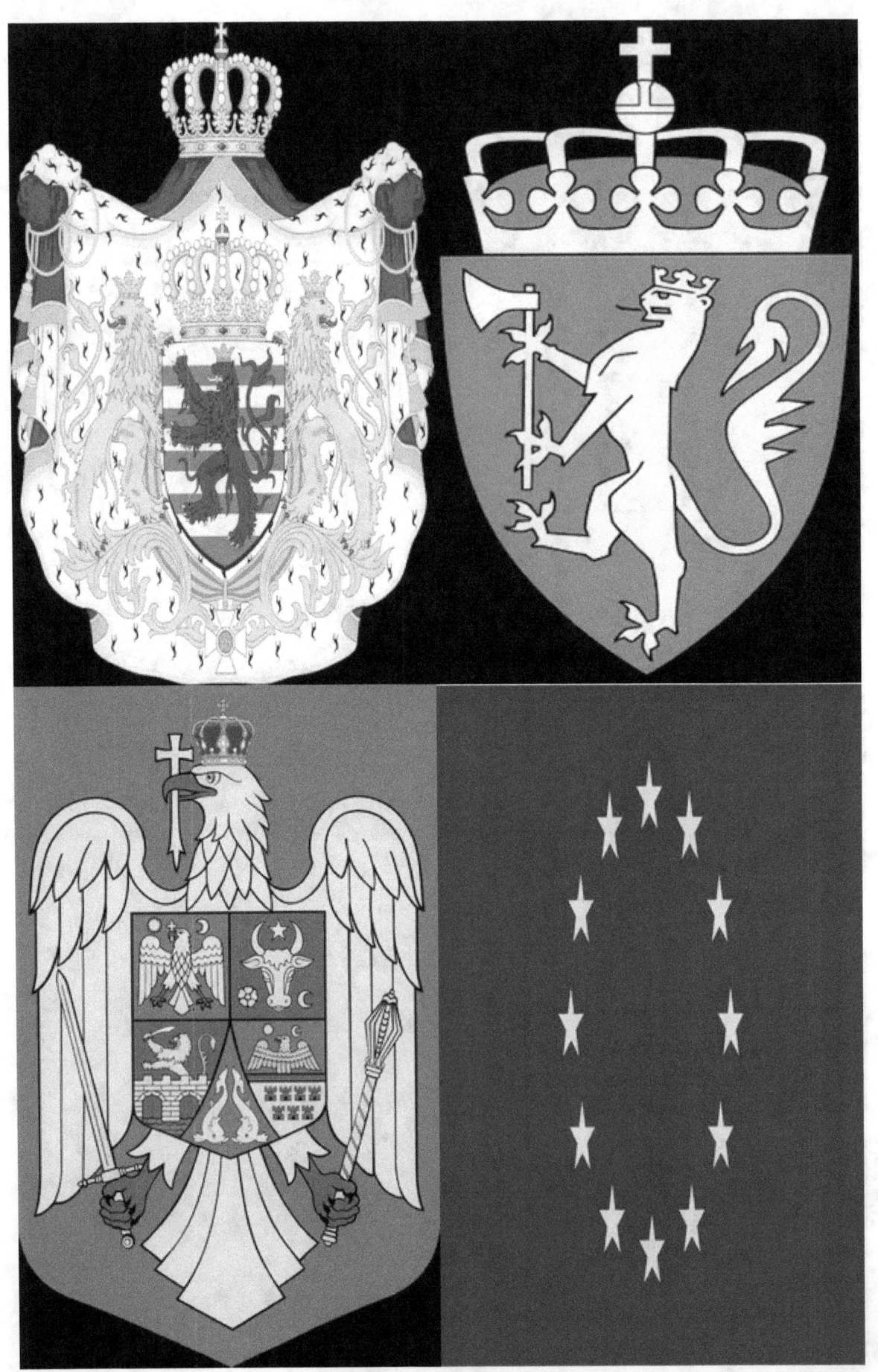

Arya Bàhram

Black Europe

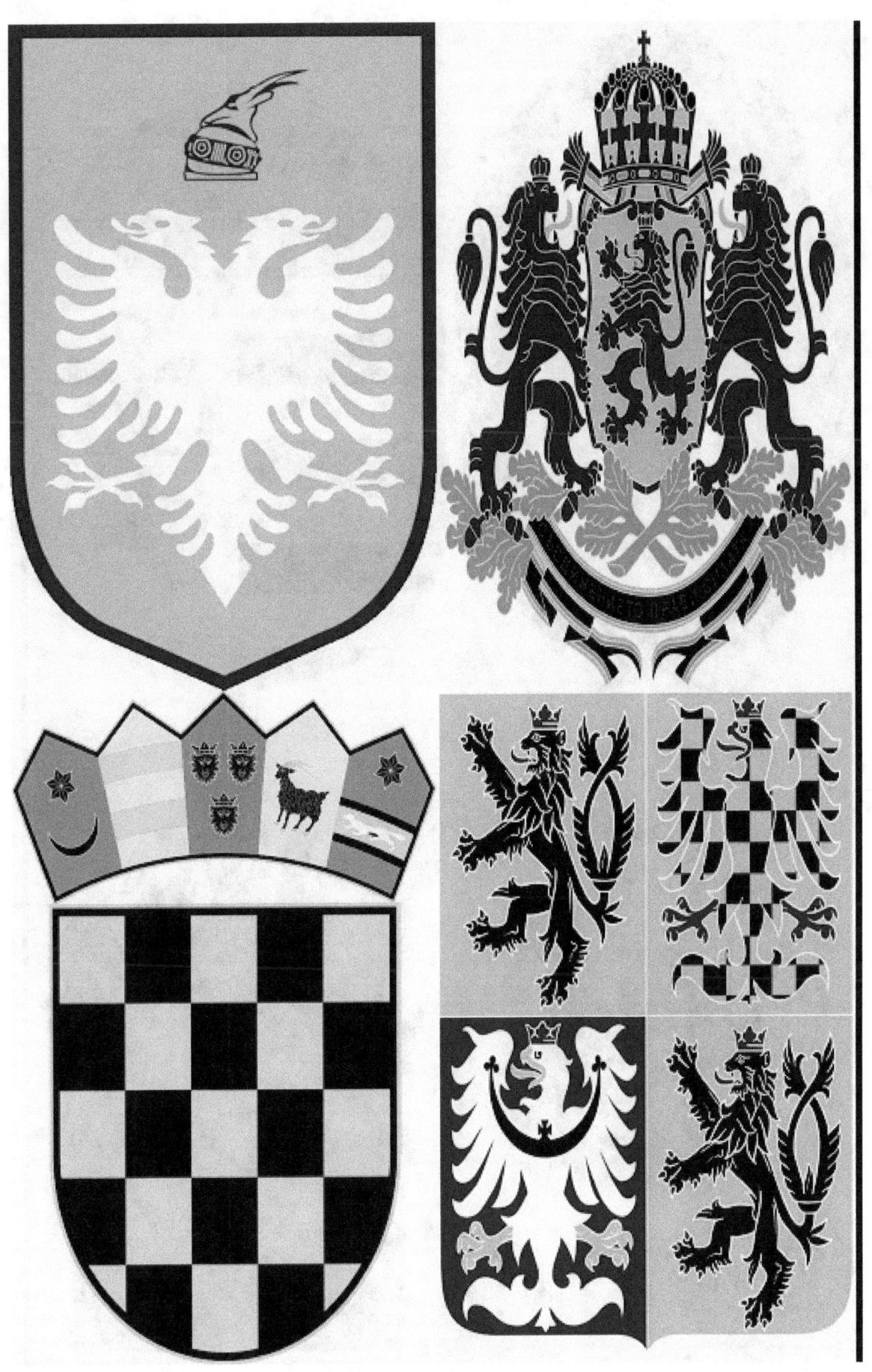

Arya Bàhram

Black Europe

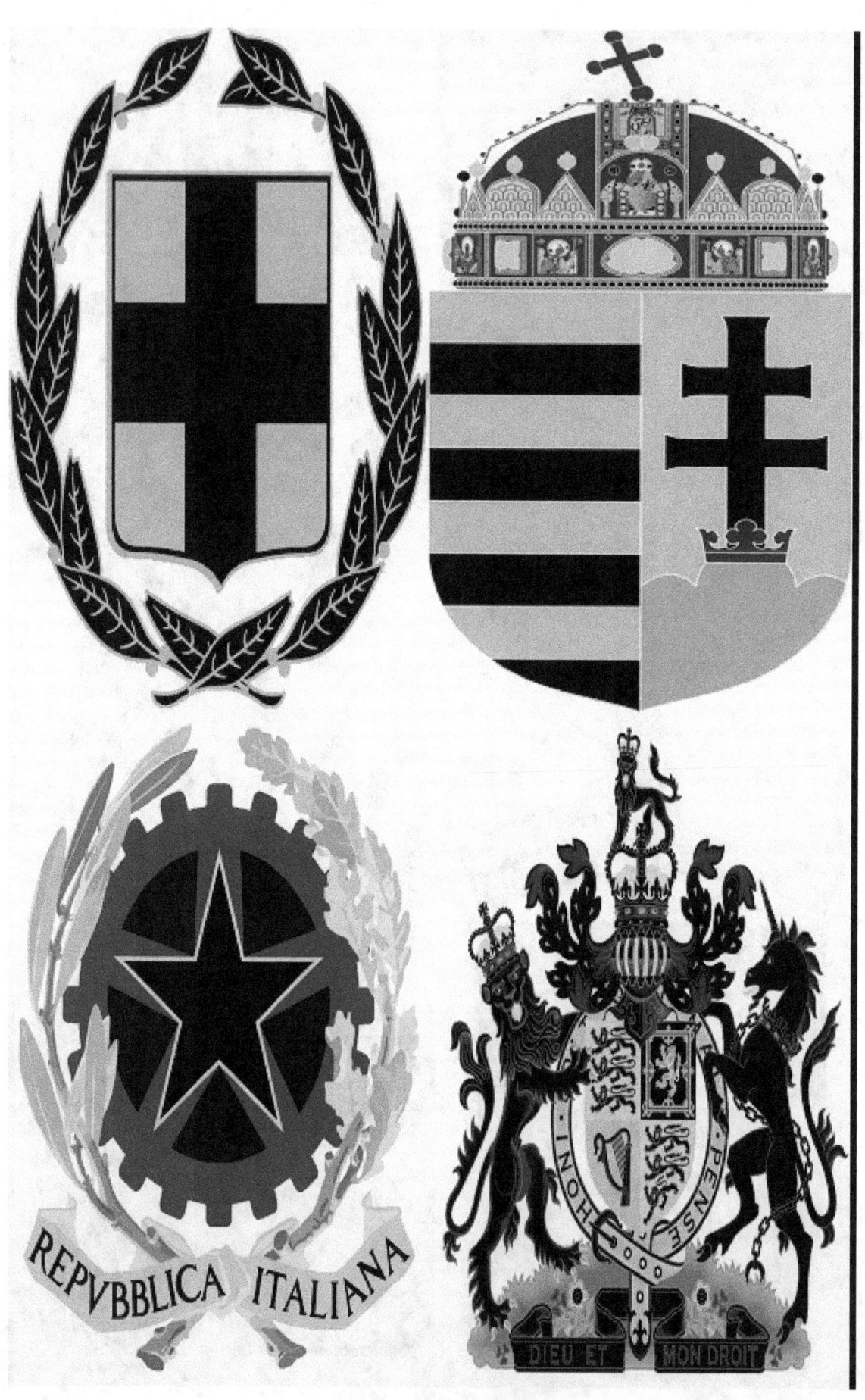

Arya Bàhram

Black Europe

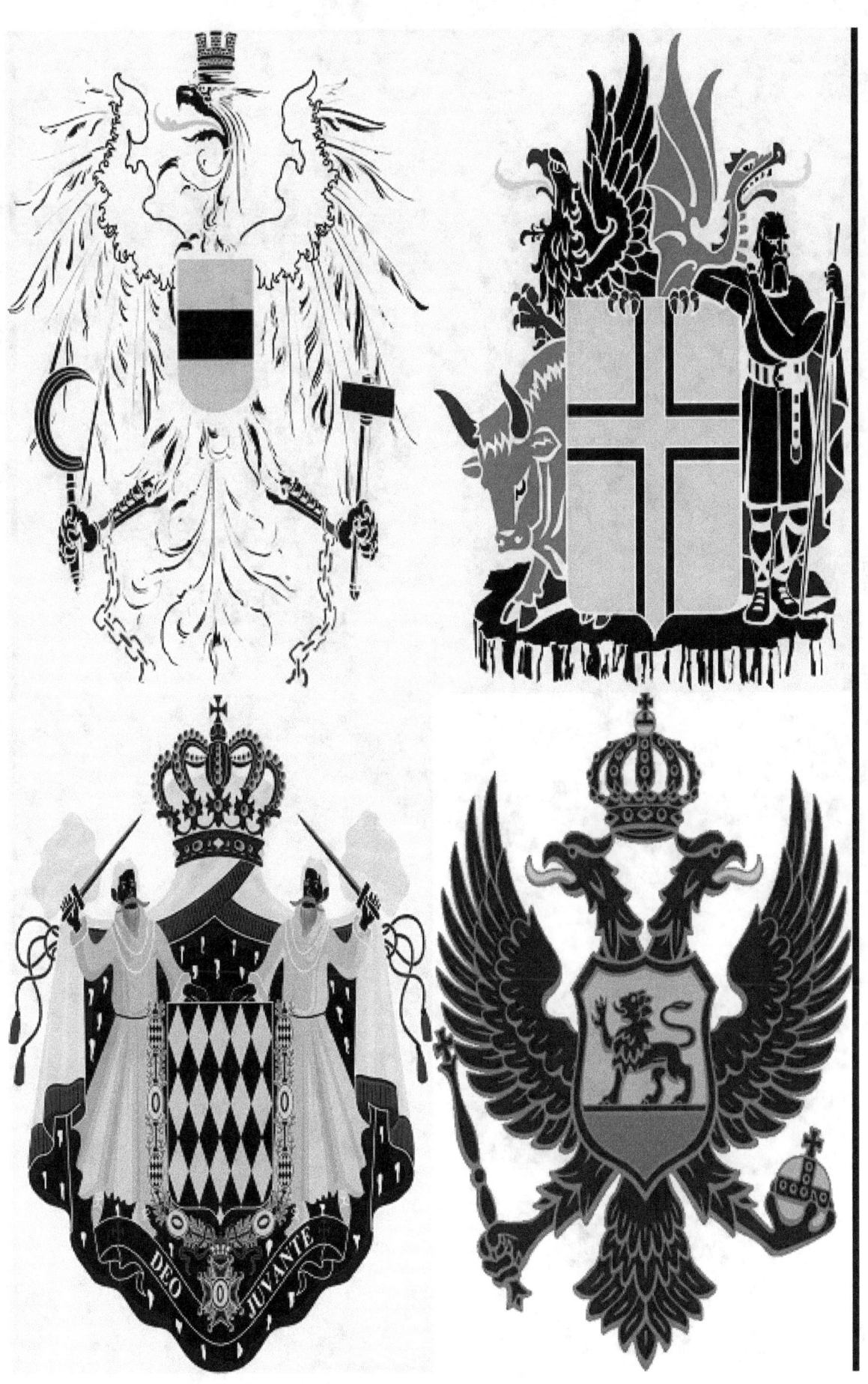

Arya Bàhram

Black Europe

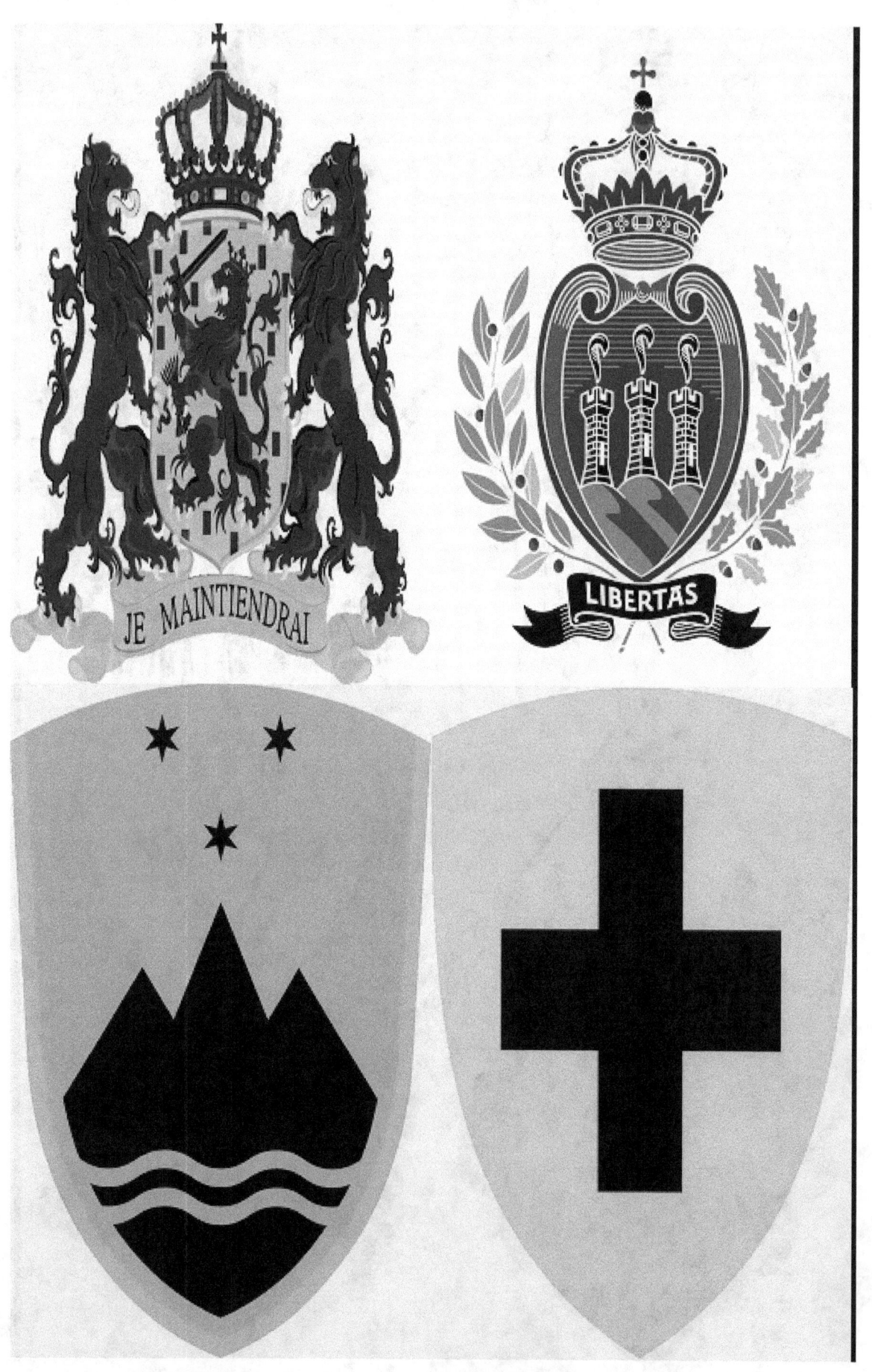

Arya Bàhram

Black Europe

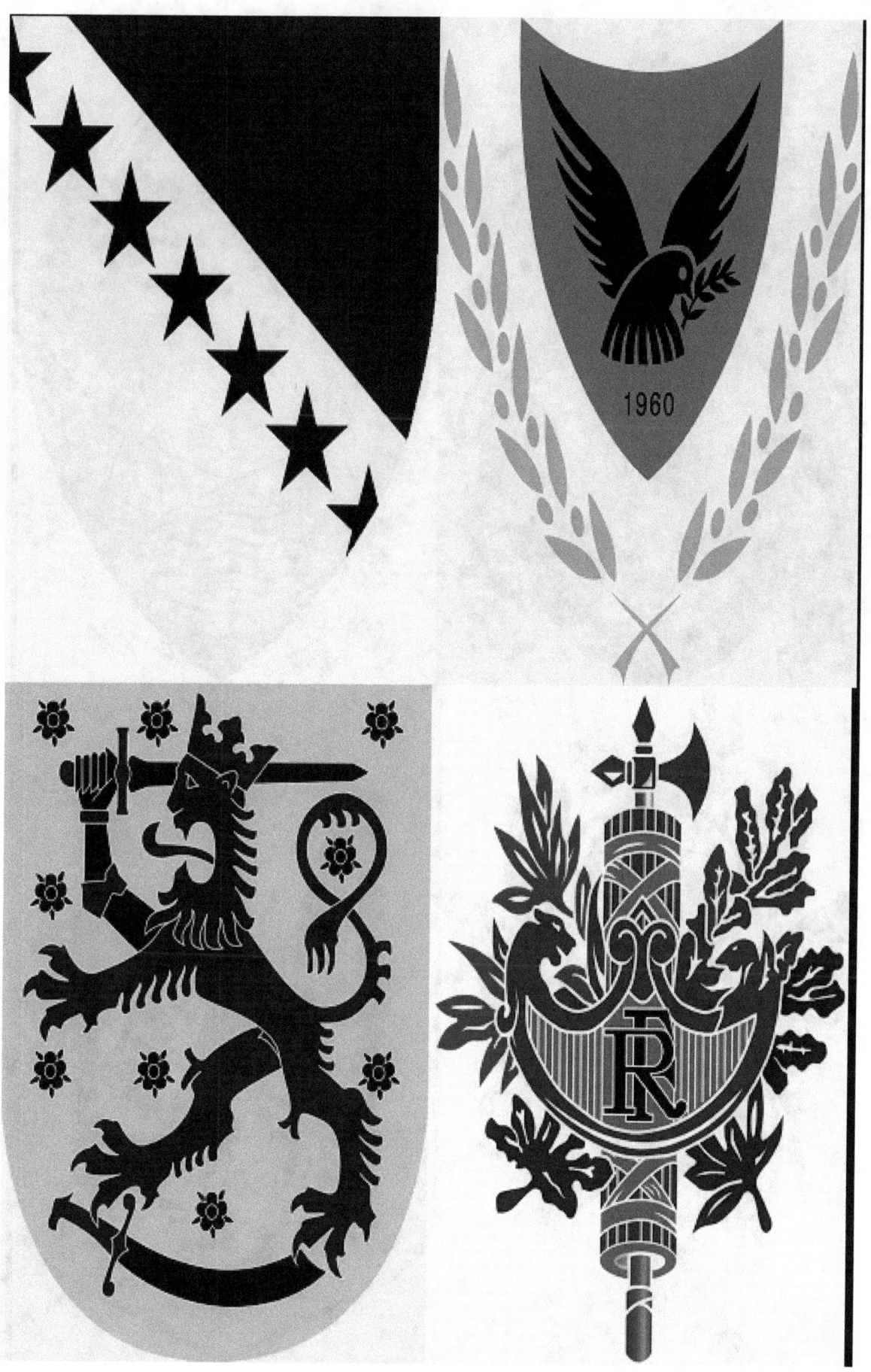

Arya Bàhram

Black Europe

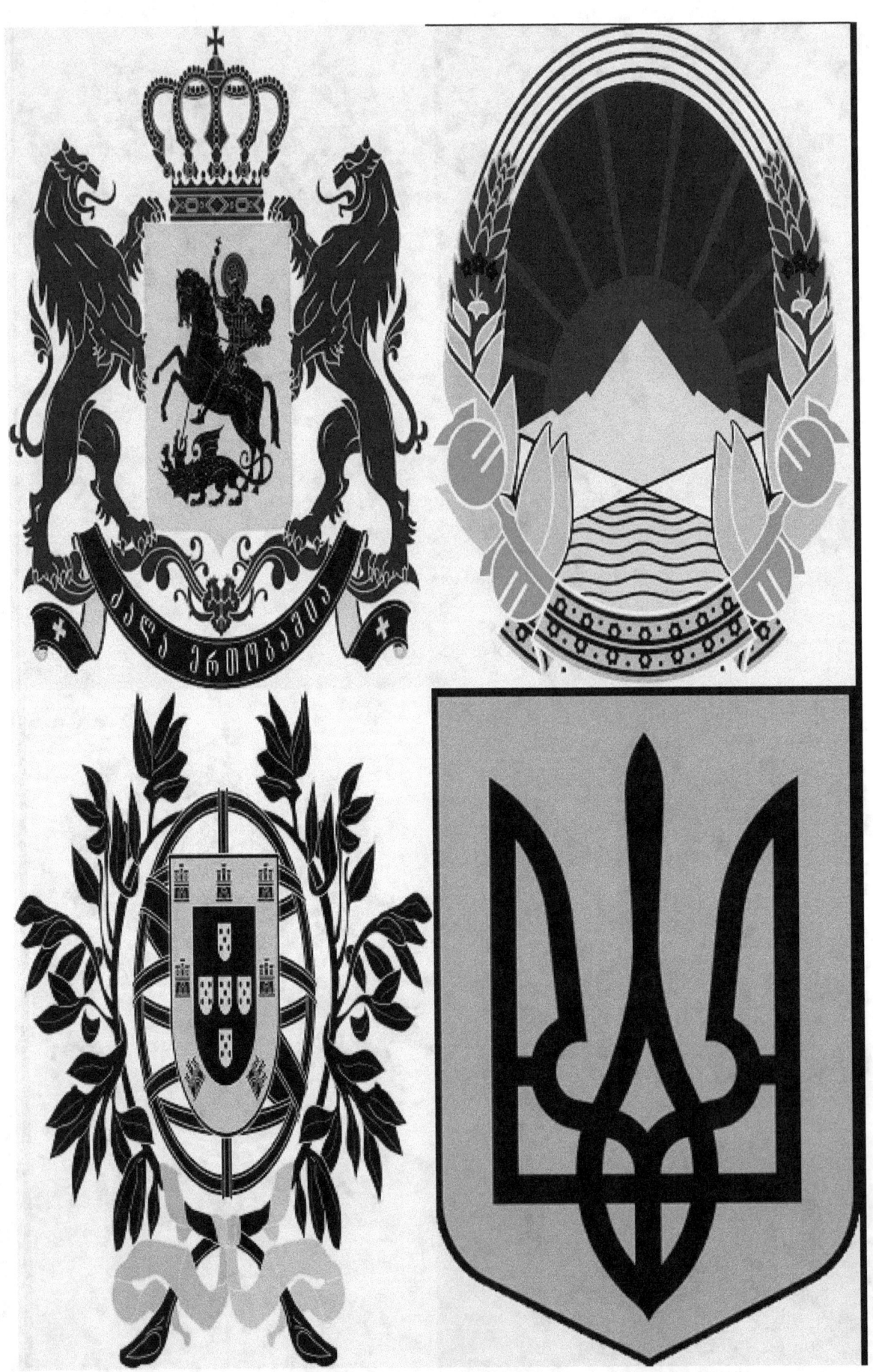

Arya Bàhram

Black Europe

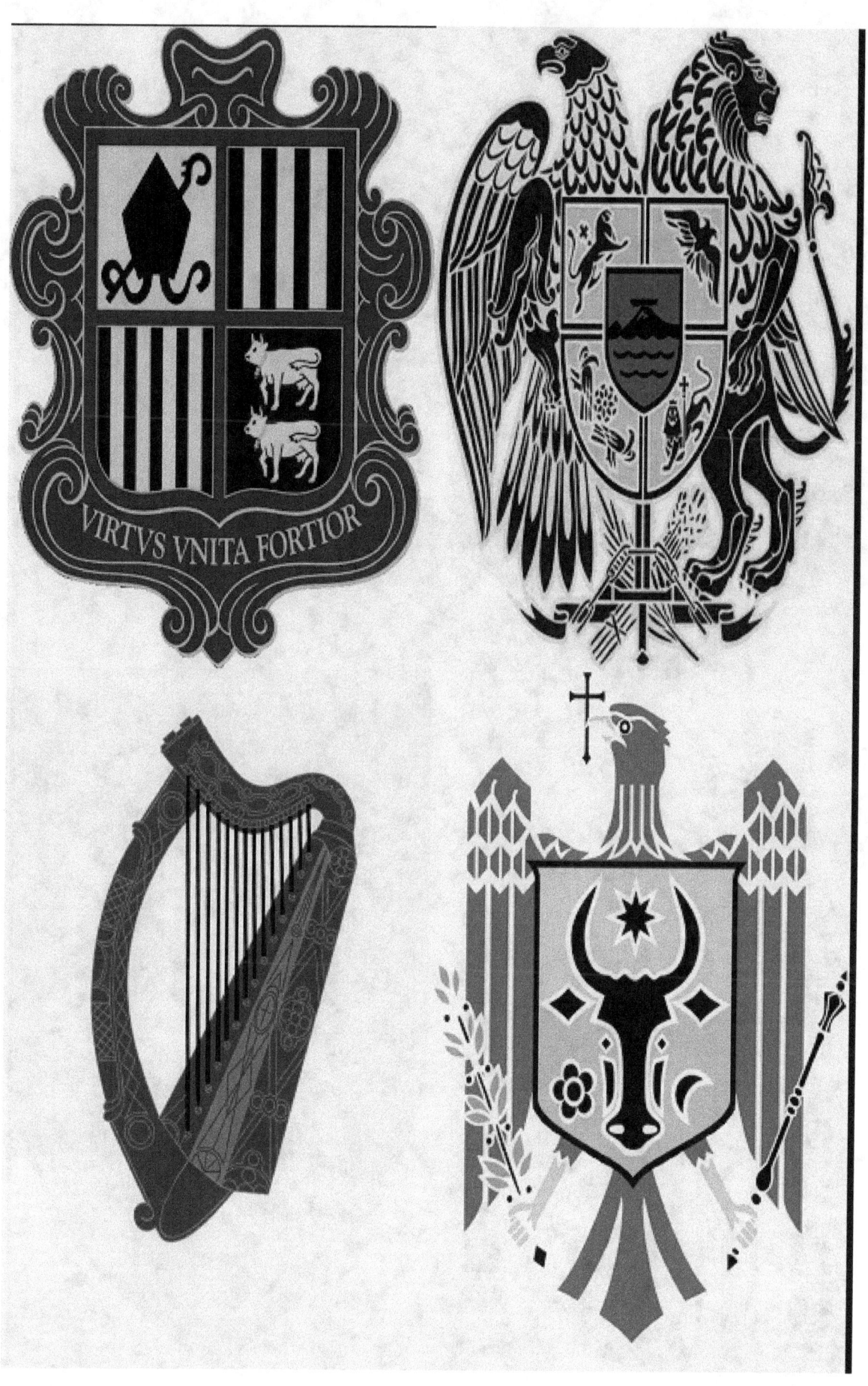

Arya Bàhram

Black Europe

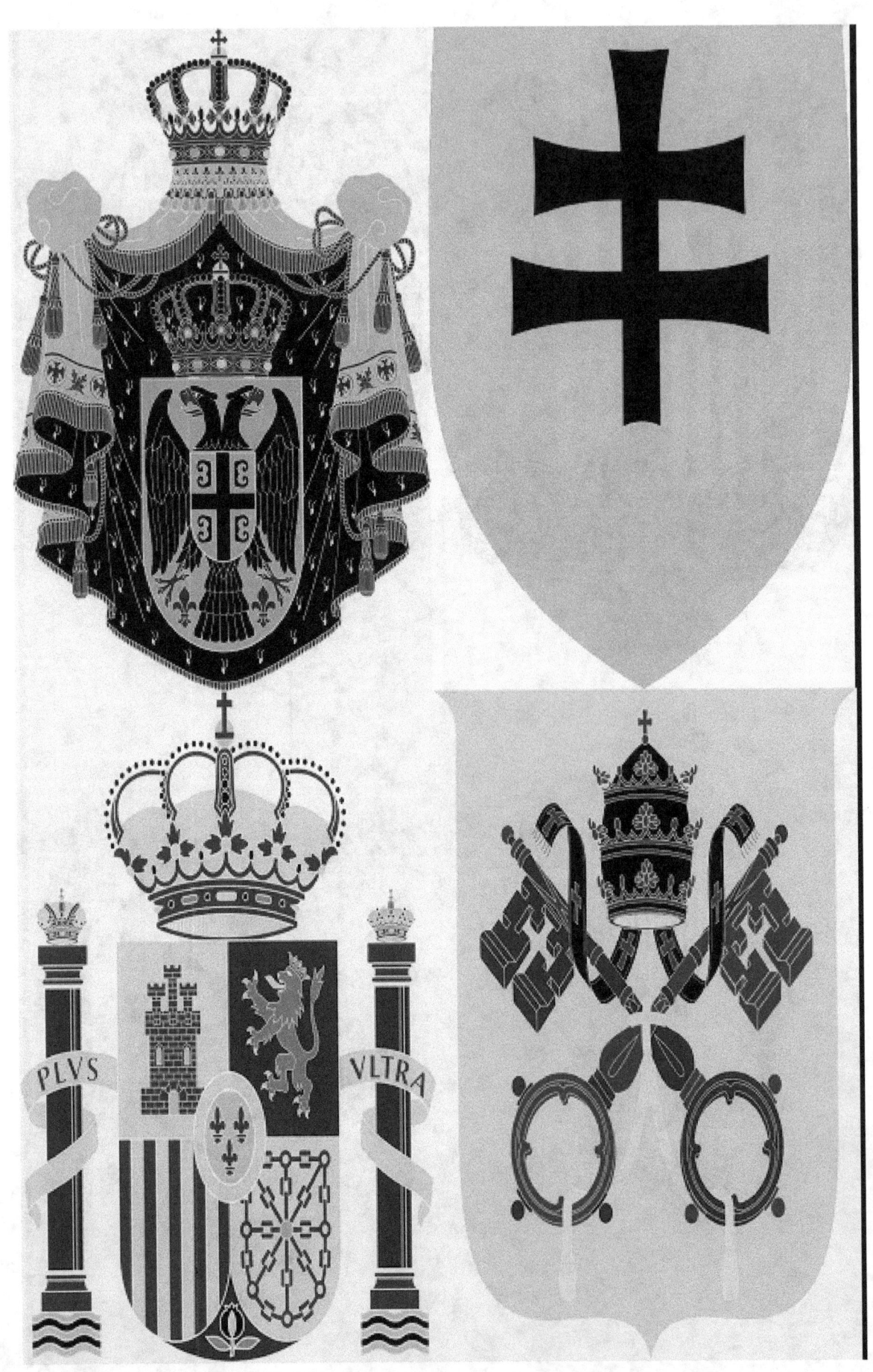

Arya Bàhram

Black Europe

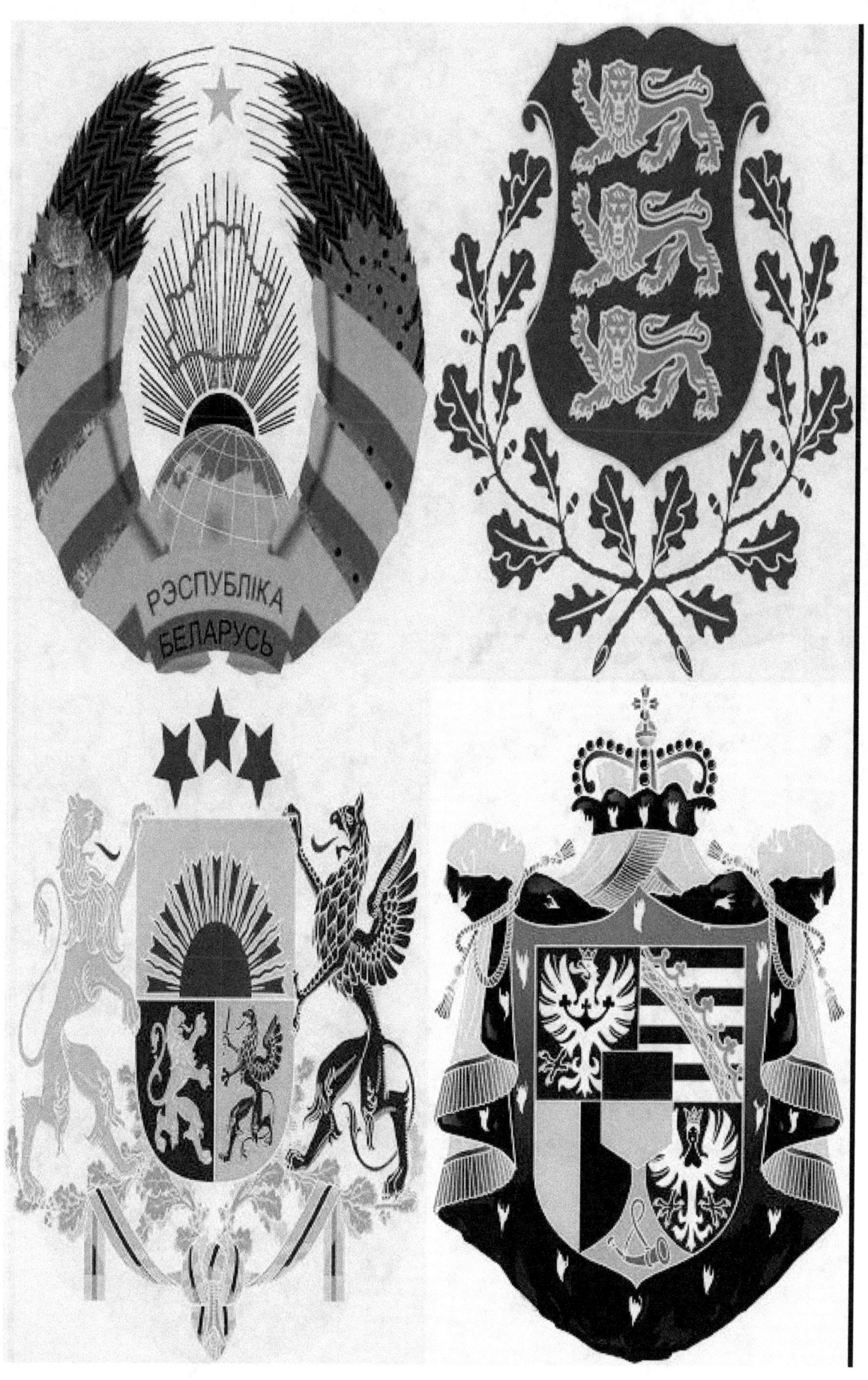

Arya Bàhram

Black Europe

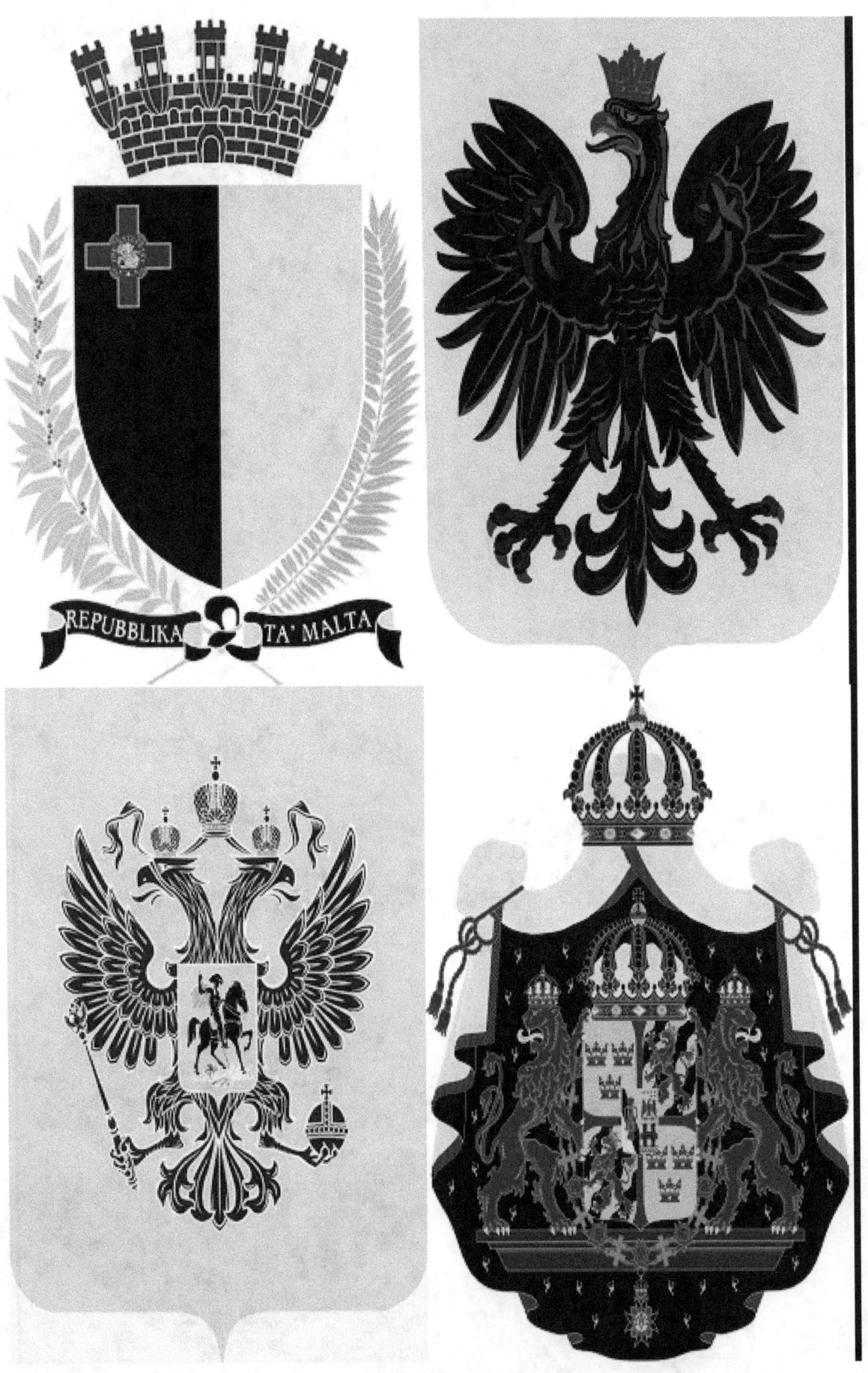

Arya Bàhram

Black Europe

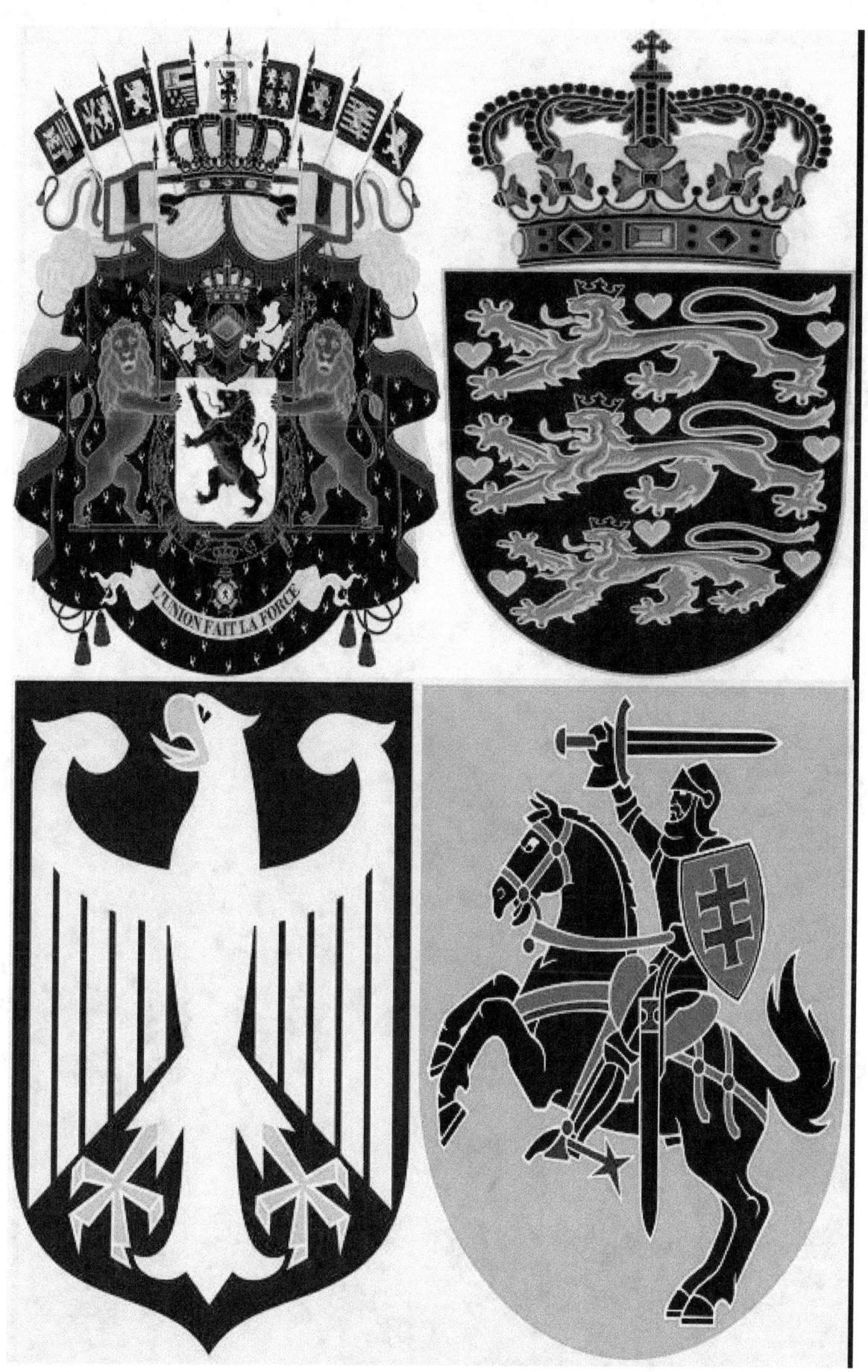

Arya Bàhram

Black Europe

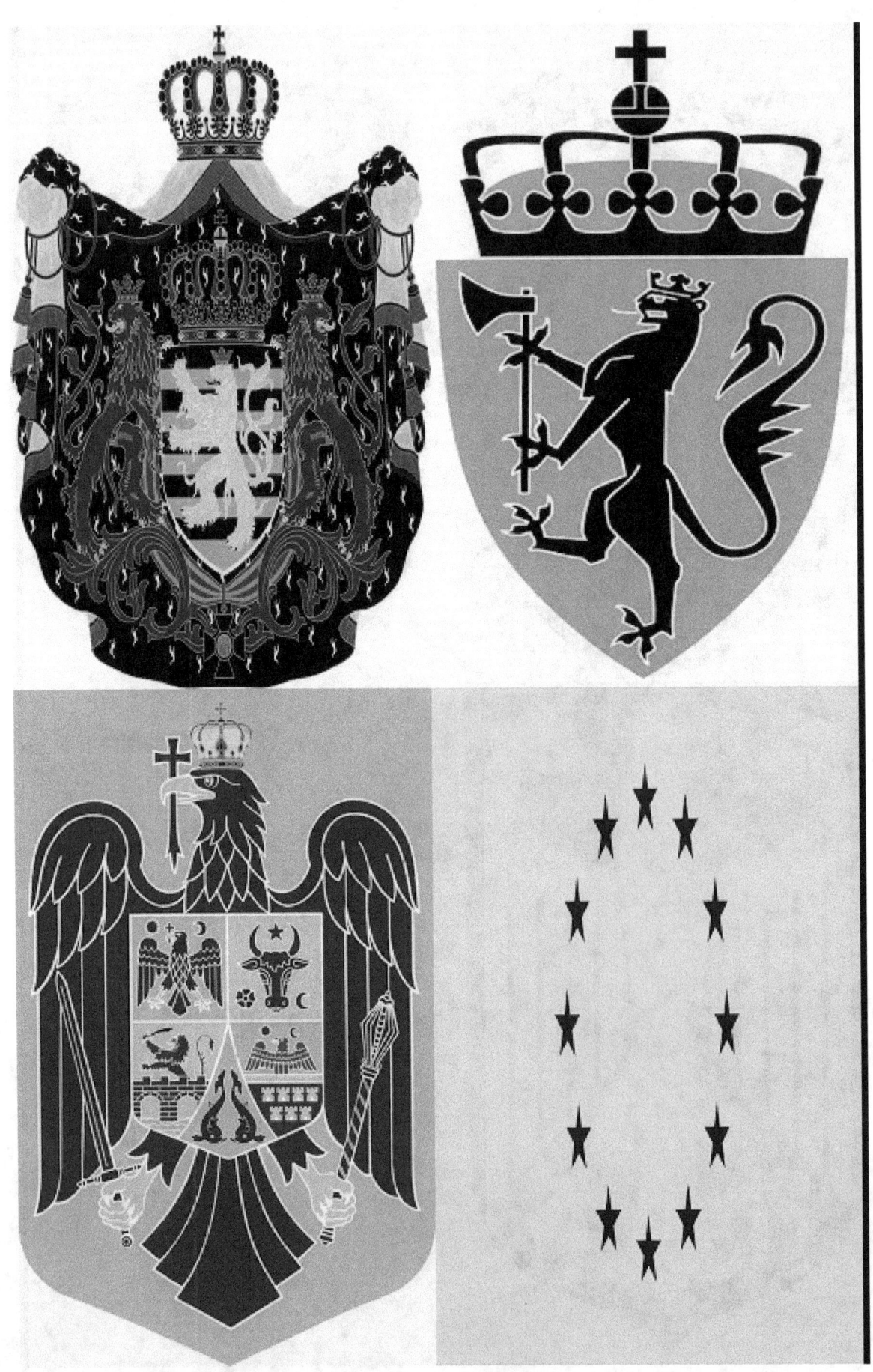

Arya Bàhram

Black Europe

Arya Bàhram

www.ingramcontent.com/pod-product-compliance
Lightning Source LLC
Chambersburg PA
CBHW081302180526
45170CB00007B/2527